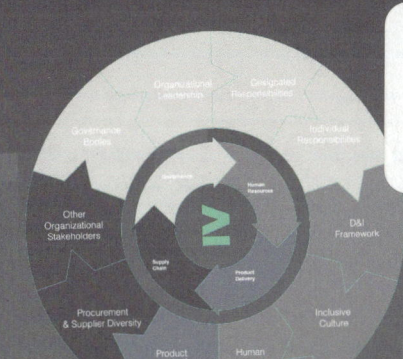

ISO-30415
DIVERSITY & INCLUSION SERVICE MANAGEMENT

JFK Keith Institute

Governance
Human Resources
Product Delivery
Supply Chain

Foundations of Diversity & Inclusion
Service Management

Based on ISO-30415

A publication of Keith Institute

COLOPHON

KEITH INSTITUTE PRESS
Published and Edited by the Keith Institute's
Corporate Ethnography & Inclusion Score Project

James Felton Keith, 2021
All Rights Reserved

Library of Congress Cataloging-in-Publication Data

Keith, James Felton
ISO-30415 Diversity & Inclusion Service Management
KeithInstitute.com/books

ISBN-: 979-8-9897914-0-8
1. Business 2. Education 3. Technology 4. Diversity

PRINTED IN THE UNITED STATES OF AMERICA
DESIGNED BY JAMES FELTON KEITH

The moral right of the author has been asserted.
All rights reserved. Without limiting the rights under copyright reserve above, all of this publication may be reproduced, stored or introduced into a retrieval system, or transmitted, in any form or by any means (electronic, mechanical, photocopying, recording or otherwise), without the prior written permission of both the copyright owner and the above publisher of this book.

FOREWORD

As my fellow human rights activists assert, pride is a protest. It is with great pride that I present this amended version of *Foundations of D&I Service Management based on ISO-30415* from our initial publication on September 25, 2021 for the use of the world's first certification class in ISO-30415 for Diversity & Inclusion (D&I). The language of D&I has scaled towards diversity equity inclusion belonging accessibility and justice, but when we write D&I throughout this text, we are referring to all of those terms no matter how widely adopted or newly argued they are in the lexicon of organizational people management.

With the long-awaited update of the International Organization for Standard's (ISO) ISO-30415®, launched in May of 2021, this ISO-30415 foundations guide had to be completely reconfigured to suit its objective: provide an easy introduction to the broad library of fragmented D&I practices as a method of corporate change management. In order to fully support the evolution of D&I as it becomes a business process, I think it necessary to acknowledge the process roots that have reshaped how the world works over the past 150 years. Starting with a man that I would otherwise despise, Frederick Winslow Taylor (1856), the American mechanical engineer and early management consultant who coined the term "scientific-management" was the most prominent of the early industrial engineers to micro-define every work task he could identify with a financial value. Fast forward to 1913 and one of his biggest clients, Ford Motor Company, establishes the first assembly line of business processes.

When I was in engineering school one of my greatest influences was industrial engineer Shigeo Shingō (1909) who created *Poka-yoke* which is a Japanese term that means "mistake-proofing" leveraged by Toyota to scale competition in the American manufacturing industry via automobiles and related devices. Shigeo, a student and critic of Frederick was first influenced by the Lean methodology of the 1940's Toyota Corporation. As autos consumed the corporate supply-chain in the middle of the 20th Century, process became king. A few decades later in the 1980s, *Six*

Sigma was established as a method of continual process improvement by Bill Smith (1929) while working at the Chicago company, Motorola. It had implications on every business process from accounting services to manufacturing products.

Fast forward again from 1987 – 1997, a panel of industrial engineers and related academics developed the Capability Maturity Model Integration (CMMI®) to improve the usability of mature processes by integrating many different models into one framework. By the end of the 20th Century every profession had become an institution of peer reviewed methods rendering most workers, *white and blue collar*, a proxy of a process limitations.

In the 2000s as a young mechanical engineer a marriage of all of these scientific management processes shaped my life. They automated, the deconstruction, the development, and the distribution of all information technology by coupling the error-proofing methods of Toyota with maturity models of Carnegie Mellon University to incentivize the extraction of all data to feed society's information technology (IT) standards. In Geneva Switzerland the international organization for standards (ISO) aimed to quantify global consensus on the qualitative measures of IT. In this century we have leveraged the ISO to define consensus on IT, Cyber Security, Environmental Stewardship, Health & Safety, and now Diversity & Inclusion (D&I).

The mechanical engineer in me is concerned with all problems as a distribution problem first. I fear that I may read like a robot, but if I do, I'm failing to solve the distribution problem of language in order for you to understand what I mean. By the time that I made it to Tuskegee University's College of Engineering every engineer-in-training (EIT) was being trained at root-cause-analysis and error-proofing, as if they worked for Shigeo. We are trained to examine the distribution of energy whether that energy is mechanical electrical or chemical. Before I knew what engineering was, growing up as a Black Queer kid in Detroit Michigan, I was concerned with how solutions to distribution problems are built. I've also been concerned with the value of those solutions. My second career as a labor economist was rooted in a realization that there were also distribution problems in socio-economics that could be solved as a business process. I became obsessed with the hope that economists could track the distribution of value in the way that engineers could track the distribution of energy.

In the 21st Century we are living in a post information page. We know what and where information is. The work is just a matter of bearing witness to all things in existence and applying a data point to those things. Data and Personal Data in particular have become the missing link to establish the ties that bind all of our productively enterprising efforts. My teams have started to work with economists to examine data as engineers examine matter. Data is not the new oil, or water, it is the new matter, and we will apply a data point to every piece of matter; further, everything that matters. I liken it to the First Law of Thermodynamics: energy cannot be created or destroyed, but can change form. Value cannot be created or destroyed, but can change form. Value, a proxy of data's transactions. Energy, a proxy of matter's friction.

Modern corporations and the distribution of capital are dependent on the phenomenon of value transaction. Specifically they require more personal data about all of us. This reality is driving economic inclusion in a seemingly natural way. It is a type of what I call *Technological Constructivism*. Before the 21st century there were two schools of thought on how society works. The Social Constructivists who thought culture drives change, and Technological Determinists who thought tech drives change. Today we can witness culture in data points and deploy the things that culture demands based on our ability to technically collect culture's data. In short, individual's data are supplying the demand that our institutions (two or more individuals) supply. We even supply the demand for more institutions. That phenomenon commands a continuous cycle of self-identifying and allowing society's gaze onto our identities. It has transformed the market of goods (products & services) and also our workforce's ability to produce goods. D&I is a proxy of the rapid identification of nearly 8 billion humans and counting.

Our work at the Keith Institute is primarily driven by that last sentence. A delivery method to include all people in the normal economy based on their input to either create products (things we can touch) or services (things we cannot touch) is the necessary infrastructure we'll require to solve the lingering distribution problem of connecting humans to the value they contribute.

This book was produced the same way other publications of the DISM Library were produced: a broad team of expert editors, expert authors and expert reviewers contributed to a comprehensive text, and a lot of effort was spent to engage D&I Professionals on their real world experiences.

James Felton Keith

Chief Editor DISM Library for Keith Institute

ACKNOWLEDGEMENTS

This publication is the result of the cooperation of many experts and students of the field, in many different countries, representing users, providers, government, trainers, examiners, and D&I Professionals (DIPs) from the DISM Forum (DISMF). It was developed as an introduction to D&I Service Management, first published on September 25, 2021 by James Felton Keith but is expanded by the broader DISMF. We would like to acknowledge the inaugural DISMF cohorts.

Prater Jasmine, Karen | Mielke, Alejandra | Thomas, Bryan | Jackson, Eric | Foreman, Cathy | Cross, Christopher | Sanchez-Cabezudo, Inigo | Pee, Crystal | Williams, Donnielle | Hoffmann, Emily | Garcia, Flor | Gatson, Brandon | Thompkins, Aisha | Skidmore, Sarah | Wade, Jonathan | Oltmanns, Julia | Heard, Kevin | Berry, LaSonya | Brown, Lisa | Guma, Zimkhitha | Spence, Margaret | Beecher, Meeckel | Robinson, Maurice | Shingane, Neha | Ekwerike, Onyedika | Adams, Patricia | Viau, Rachel | Esparza, Raul | Fugett, Russell | Dotson, Tai | Sears, Tamica | Sibert, Tony | Beba, Umran | Pineyro, Venus | Learned-Fenty, Victoria | Dillard, Whitnee | Ayers, Benjamin | Brown, Sharnice | Jones, Lindsay | Storey, Adam | Harris, Alondra | Hammonds, Alicia | Smith, Alijah | D'Angelo, Amy | Daley, Andre | Williams, Blaine | Matlack, Brian | Crumbley, Carl | Pollonais, Christina | Waltzman, David | Prince, Dexter | Webb, Dion | Moghimi, Floria Susan | Swann, Gaynelle | Moreno, Gina | Iglehart, Hope | Miller Evans, Janet | Nwasike, Joan | Suber, Jon | Davis, Judith | Gross, Kevin | Hardy, Kevin | Colbert, Monikka | Web, Meshea | Cunningham, Michael | Schutz, Mike | Harris, Petina | Barbee, Quiana | Rund, Rebekah | Booker, Robert | James, Terri | Johnson, Bill | Damchevski, Aleksandar | Chisolm-Noel, Anadri | Elliott, Ashley | Brown, Audrey | Darden, Byron | Bisanzio, Christiane | Vaughn, David | Swink, Dawn | Joseph, Edna | Scheffres Watts, Elizabeth | Srinivas, Jaya | Wells, Denise | Espinosa Valencia, Linda | Garcia, Louise | Smith-Pope, LaShaunda | Beltas, Maelle | Fenton, Mark | Leach, Mary Jane | Beckley, Margaret | Viswanath, Megha | Heyward, Michele | Taylor, Nicole | Bance, Shereen | Hampton, Stephanie | Burden, Timothy | Ellis,

Toni | Pointer, Tracy | Cortese, Amy | Desmaison Cornejo, Ana Maria | HASAN, ATIYA | Smith, Barbara Holmes | Moncrief, Brandi | Malone, Christianne | Williams, Christopher | Haggard, Eric | Schmid, Emily | Townsend MPPM, Gregory | Wollack-Spiller, Geronda | Mubiru, Ipolito | Greene, Israel | Bekele, Jaly | Peters, Jan | Jones, Kim | Condyles, Mark | Gibson, Meg | Vasser, Mia | Muñoz, Paula | Leibnitz, Gretalyn | De Crée, Carl | Fletcher, Rachel | Opeka, Radly | Guinn, Regina | Fatzynytz, Richard | de Jesus das Neves, Rosangela | Foster, Sheri | Sillitto, Sarah | Williams, Tonya | Hofman-Bennett, Whitney | Shotlow-Hatchell, Windy | Landers-Potts, Melissa | Benson, Mayowa | Bi, Paul | Bylone, Christopher | Chenier, Lois | Claiborne, John | Crowder, Curtis | Crum, Otis | Cyrus, Gino | Dial, Jackie | DiCostanza, Aenoy | Duncan, Ronnie | Epps, Remy | Feliciano, Elyssa | Hill, Orlando | Holder, Tonya | HORTON, SHYLECIA | Johnson, Tamra | King-Byous, Toni | Kombat, Kelli | Lundy, Rae | Maxwell, Bailey | McGlothen, Cameron | Mosquera Rosado, Ana Lucia | Patel, Anita | Plant, B Andrew | Premazzi, Viviana | Priest, Bryan | Rabiu, Adesiji | Radley, Jana | Roberts, Stacy | Sergent, Gary | Smith, Kimberly | Stenson, Iman | Thomas, Tres | Underwood, Leah | Volk, Melissa | Wardlaw, David | White, Elise | Woma, Sharon | Bailey, Julian | Ballina, Scott | Burkes, Carolyn | Chapman, Mary | Cho, Mi | Cook, Kristen | Crew, Annesia | Dortschy, Kristina | Flynn, Patti | Hamacher, Ruby | Iverson, Mara | Jongerius, Olla | Klinger, Maira | Leyton, Katie | Lopez, Adrian | Reid, Denise | Rosado, Kathy | Salazar, Abel | Sen, Indranil | Smith, Shon | Sowa, Megan | Vaughan, Nicholas | Walker, Horace | Weaver, Tenise | Yordanov, Deniz

Given the desire for a broad consensus in the D&I Service Management field, new developments, additional material and contributions from DISM professionals who have worked with ISO-30415 are welcome. They will be discussed by the editors via the DISM Forum1 and where appropriate incorporated into new editions. Comments can be sent to the Chief Editor of the DISM Library

CONTENTS

COLOPHON 4
FOREWORD 5
ACKNOWLEDGEMENTS 9

CHAPTER 1 NTRODUCTION 13
   1.1 Background 13
   1.2 Why this book 15
   1.3 Organizational History 15
   1.4 Structure of the book 19
   1.5 How to use this book 21

PART 1 DIVERSITY & INCLUSION INFRASTRUCTURE LIBRARY 23

CHAPTER 2 INTRODUCTION TO THE DISM LIFECYCLE 25

   2.1 Introduction 25
   2.2 Four D&I Project Categories 26
   2.3 Twenty-Seven Diversity Types 28
   2.4 Thirty-Two Domains of Diversity and Inclusion ... 48
   2.5 ISO References and Definitions 49
   2.6 Governance 58
   2.7 Diversity and Inclusion (D&I) Framework 62
   2.8 Inclusive Culture 64
   2.9 Human Resources Management Lifecycle (HRMLC) ... 68
   2.10 Product and Services Development and Delivery ... 85
   2.11 Supply Chain and Other Stakeholders 88

PART 2 DIVERSITY & INCLUSION SERVICE DELIVERY 93

CHAPTER 3 SERVICE PORTFOLIOS & SERVICE CATALOGUES 95

   3.1 Service Portfolio Management 95
   3.2 Service Catalogue Management 99
   3.3 Service Catalogue Use Case 104

CHAPTER 4 INCLUSION MATURITY MODEL INTEGRATION 107

4.1 Introduction 107
4.2 2021-23 Inclusion Maturity Model Integration 114
4.3 Benefits and Risks of DISM Frameworks 117
4.4 Benefits 118
4.5 Methods Techniques, and Tools 125
4.6 Implementation 136

**CHAPTER 5 FUNCTIONS AND PROCESSES IN
SERVICE OPERATION 153**

5.1 Event Management 153
5.2 Incident Management 161
5.3 Request Fulfillment 170
5.4 Problem Management 174
5.5 Access Management 184
5.6 Monitoring and Control 189
5.7 D&I Operations 196
5.8 D&I Service Desk 199

INDEXING 206

CHAPTER 1
INTRODUCTION

1.1 BACKGROUND

In the United States of America and the Western World an evolution of D&I has kept pace with changes in the demographic of wage earning individuals. In 2023 the most common argument for D&I is one rooted in marketing, and meeting the demand of inclusion equity and belonging in an increasingly diverse population. A few factors cater to this reality.

1. The growth rate of educated women
2. The increased migration to and expansion of cities
3. The on-slot of personal data and the micro-identification of individual identities

In the words of the author of the first employment law text book, Dawn Bennett-Alexander, "we strive to embrace diversity and inclusion in our schools and workplaces, but we often fail to understand what this looks like practically". D&I have meant different things to different organizations over the past seven (7) decades, as it should. D&I is not only institutional, it is individual, it is regional, and it is specific to every business model. The distribution of D&I has increased as multi-national corporations and government alliances have increased into the 21st Century. Still our origins are rooted in the struggle to sign into law **Title VII of the Civil Rights Act of 1964**. Title VII, as amended, protects employees and job applicants from employment discrimination based on race, color, religion, sex and national origin.

Case law in the Western World has expanded discrimination to retaliation or forms of whistle blowing from inside of organizations of all types: for-profit, non-profit, and governments. Further, every corporation is an extension of the corpus, or the lives that make up its 2 or more member-parts. As a result they are subject to more and more ethical considerations when engaging individual stakeholders of varied types, not just individual employees.

This growth in what case law can be used for coupled with both the streamlining of human resources practices and integration of demographics, have created our new normal. Progress is seemingly slow, but it often catches organizations and their norms off guard. In 1948 the Society for Human Resources Management (SHRM) was founded and the first employment law book was published in 1995. More than twenty years later, the addition of a global consensus like the ISO-30415 standard is a commencement standardization. We are finally at a place where D&I can become a profession at industrial scale through the normal processes of critiquing maturity and rigor using the same language across many locales. This has been necessary in every of type of business service to achieve sustainable success in organizational culture.

1.2 WHY THIS BOOK

Other than this book being rooted in explaining the standard for D&I in a methodological way, this book offers detailed information for those who are responsible for strategic inclusion efforts, as well as for the (much larger) group who are responsible for setting up and executing the delivery of the D&I across an organization. This is supported by both the description of the D&I Framework, as documented in ISO-30415:2021, and by the description of the processes that are associated with it. The ISO-30415 core elements are very extensive, and can be used for a thorough study of contemporary best practices. This Foundations book provides the reader with an easy-to-read comprehensive introduction to the broad library of ISO-30415 core elements, to support the understanding and the further distribution of ISO-30415 as the industrialization of inclusion commences. Once this understanding of the structure of ISO-30415 has been gained, the reader can use the core elements for a more detailed understanding and guidance for their daily D&I practices.

1.3 ORGANIZATIONAL HISTORY

Several organizations and thousands of individuals were involved in the origination of ISO-30415 as a description of the 'best practice' to deliver Diversity & Inclusion.

2010

The first work was commissioned by the Society for Human Resources Management (SHRM) and Cari Dominguez, the former head of the Equal Employment Opportunity Commission (EEOC) was tapped to lead the working group.

The group established three (3) working teams focused on Diversity Programs, Competencies for Top Diversity Professionals, and Diversity Metrics.

2014

The group completed draft recommendations for SHRM. However, SHRM decided to suspend its work on human resources (HR) standards in late 2014. The three work groups were advised to stop. At that time Effenus Henderson and Lorelei Carobolante decided to pursue a diversity & inclusion (D&I) standard through the International Organization for Standards (ISO) in Geneva, Switzerland.

2015

At the ISO Effenus Henderson and Lorelei Carobolante submitted a new work proposal to establish a global D&I standard.

2016

The proposal was approved in May of 2016 an Working Group 8 (WG8) was established in October of 2016. WG8 was and remains a subcommittee of ISO Technical Committee (TC) ISO/TC 260 Human Resource Management (HRM), Henderson was elected by the TC to serve as Convener and Carobolante was elected to serve as Co-Convener/project leader. The first WG8 meeting was held in December of 2016.

The international working group consisted of experts, consultants, and practitioners from around the world. The group sought input as several drafts of the proposed standard was shared for commenting across all of the member nations of the ISO. Over 700 comments recommending changes to the standard were reviewed and addressed by the working group.

2020

In 2020, the working group completed its development of the proposal after a series of refinements based on standardized ISO reviews.

2021

The standard was submitted for a final vote in early 2021 and was approved in April of 2021 and subsequently published in May of 2021. The standard, officially names ISO Standard 30415:2021, was the first global guidance standard for diversity and inclusion adopted by the ISO.

The ISO-30415 Standard has also been adopted as a contribution method to the United Nations Sustainable Development Goals, 10 for Reduced Inequalities, 8 for Decent Work and Economic Growth , and 5 for Gender Equality.

DISMF

The target group for this publication is anyone who is involved or interested in D&I Service Management. A professional organization, working on the development of the D&I Service Management field, has been created especially for this target group.

In 2021 the Diversity & Inclusion Service Management Forum (DISMF) was built out of the early cohorts of professionals certified in the ISO-30415:2021 standard at the University of Georgia's Terry College of Business in tandem with a global Insurance Industry D&I Roundtable established to scrutinize the deployment of people management via the tool of D&I domains listed in the ISO standard.

Since then, independent DISMF participants have been set up in more than fourteen countries, spread across the globe, and the numbers continues to grow. All DISMF participants operate under the umbrella organization, Keith Institute.

DISMF is aimed at the entire professional area of D&I Service Management. It promotes the exchange of information and experiences that D&I organizations can use to improve their service provision. DISMF is also involved in the use and quality of the various standards and methods that are important in the field. One of these standards is ISO-

30415 in agreement with the ISO, British Standards Institute (BSI), and the U.S.A.'s National Science Foundation (NSF).

> *The D&I Service Management **Forum (DISMF)** is a global, independent, internationally recognized not-for-profit program of the Keith Institute dedicated to D&I Service Management. DISMF is wholly owned and principally run by its membership. It consists of a growing number of national chapters, each with a large degree of autonomy, but adhering to a common code of conduct The DISMF is a major influence on, and contributor to, industry best practices and standards worldwide, working in partnership with a wide, international range of governmental and standards bodies.*
>
> *Keith Institute is the controlling body of the DISMF national chapters and sets policies and provides direction for furthering the overall objectives of DISMF, for the adoption of D&I Service Management (DISM) best practice and for ensuring adherence to DISMF policies and standards.*

This Foundations book is a publication of Keith Institute, published in the DISM Library series. The book fits in well with the mission of Keith Institute:

> ***The mission of Keith Institute** is to foster education and economic inclusion. That mission is the core incentive for Keith Institute to establish methods that incentivize a dynamic adoption of the most modern methods of inclusion across all global organization types.*

This mission can be translated into the following publishing activities:

> **DISMF Publishing activities:**
>
> > *publishing supporting material on accepted best practice*
> > *publishing material that represents 'new thought' in the DISM field*
> > *ensuring that, through all activities, including the publication of relevant material, DISMF assists organizations in the implementation of solutions that will deliver real value to them*

By publishing this detailed introduction to the field of D&I Service Management, based on ISO-30415, Keith Institute offers a valuable contribution to the development of the subject.

EXAM BODIES

The Inclusion Corporation (Inclusion Score Incorporated) and the University of Georgia's Terry College of Business are the earliest to provide development and provision of certification for D&I Service Management, in 2021. For many years since the publication of the ISO-30415:2021 standard they were the only bodies that provided ISO-30415 exams. Together and separately they have certified individuals Diversity & Inclusion Professionals (DIPs) across five (5) continents.

1.4 STRUCTURE OF THE BOOK

This book starts with an introduction on the backgrounds and general principles of D&I Service Management and the context for ISO-30415 (**Chapter 1**). It describes the parties involved in the development of best practices and standards for D&I Service Management, and the basic premises and standards that are used.

The body of the book is set up in two large Parts: **Part 1** deals with the definitions of the D&I Infrastructure Library (DIIL), **Part 2** deals with the various service management functions and processes that can deploy and measure DISM.

Part 1 starts with **Chapter 2**, introducing the D&I Infrastructure Library as a collection of the 32 D&I Domains of the ISO-30415 standard, the 27 Diversity Types based on evolving information of protected classes of people across the industrialized world, and the 4 Project Types which service as the services to be deployed throughout the 32 Domains per the 27 Diversity Types.

In Part 2 starting with **Chapter 3**, each of the phases in the Service Lifecycle is discussed in detail, in a standardized structure: Service Strategy, Service Design, Service Transition, Service Operation and Continual Service Improvement. These chapters provide a detailed view on the characteristics of the Service Lifecycle, its construct and its elements. The main points of each phase are presented in a consistent way to aid readability and clarity, so that the text is clear and its readability is promoted. Each section follows a consistent structure:

> Introduction
> Basic concepts
> Processes and other activities
> Organization
> Methods, techniques and tools
> Implementation

The **Appendices** provide useful sources for the reader. A Reference list of used sources is provided, as well as the official ISO-30415 Glossary. The book ends with an extensive Index of relevant terms, that will support the reader in finding relevant text elements.

1.5 HOW TO USE THIS BOOK

Readers who are primarily interested in the Infrastructure Library can focus on Part 1 of the book, and pick whatever they need on functions and service processes of part 2.

Readers who are primarily interested in the functions and processes and are not ready for a lifecycle approach yet, or who prefer a process approach, can read the introductory chapters, and then focus on the functions and processes of their interest.

Readers who want a thorough introduction to ISO-30415, exploring its scope and main characteristics, can read Part 1 on the Lifecycle, and add as many of the functions and processes from Part 2 as they need or like.

In this way, this new edition of the Foundations book aims to provide support to a variety of approaches to D&I Service Management based on ISO-30415.

PART 1

DIVERSITY & INCLUSION INFRASTRUCTURE LIBRARY

CHAPTER 2
INTRODUCTION TO THE DISM LIFECYCLE

2.1 INTRODUCTION

Diversity & Inclusion Service Management (DISM)

Instead of the normal introduction that covers the history of the standard and how we got here, the fledgling nature of D&I as a service management process demands that we start with the two question that compelled the international standardization effort: where do I start? & what do I do next? – Change and further, change management is a critique of "how" not "what".

The DISM lifecycle is based on a series of questions derived from the 171 D&I Elements or 32 D&I Domains or 4 D&I Categories which give direction to Organizational Governance, Human Resources, Product Delivery, and Supplier Diversity. Each of the 32 Domains is capable of deploying one or many of the 4 D&I Project Categories as a service. The 4 Project Categories are Training, Data Extraction, Internal Infrastructure, and External Infrastructure. Each of the 4 Project types can be applies across all 27 Diversity Types, which are protected classes in one or more of the 163 countries that recognize the International Organization for Standards (ISO).

AGAIN:

The 32 Domains house one or more of the 27 Diversity Types that provide one or more of the 4 Project Types.

> *Part 2 if you would like to skip the definitions of terms in D&I and answer the two (2) questions: where do I start? And what do I do next?, go to Part 2 of this text.*

Developing an inclusive workplace requires an ongoing commitment to Diversity and Inclusion (D&I) to address real or perceived inequalities in organizational systems, policies, processes, and practices .

2.2 FOUR D&I PROJECT CATEGORIES

We often hear that D&I is people powered or people centered, and that is an objective more than a function. DISM for ISO-30415 is a framework for functionality. In order to get D&I to function, we have to make it process centered and avoid delegating extraordinary tasks to extraordinary employees alone. They can't fix us. In fact, every other facet of corporate change management endeavors to limit subjectivity of people's roles, so that any individual can enter a position and perform by design. That design can be critiqued and changed via the normal management process to explore or achieve objectives. D&I should follow this norm.

If your organization has implemented any D&I content in the past 40 years, it has been in 1 or many of thew 4 Project Types. Later in this text as we discuss Service Catalogs, we will reference these 4 types of projects that are critical to being deployed by the ISO standard.

TRAINING

Training is a straight forward terminology that represents any type of engagement that educated the body of stakeholders, both internal and external to the organization. Examples of this are:

- Bias Training
- Cultural Training
- Continued Education

DATA EXTRACTION (DE)

DE represents any type of personal data or data gathering efforts, both voluntary and involuntary, and where stakeholders (including employees) are either aware or unaware of the data collection. Examples of this are:

- Demographic Data
- Sentiment Analysis
- Market Data

INTERNAL INFRASTRUCTURE (II)

II represents the formal or informal development of internal organizational bodies that can execute accountability and design internal policies for deploying other D&I project types. Examples of this are:

- Employee Resource Groups
- Internal Advisory Boards
- Business Resource Groups

EXTERNAL INFRASTRUCTUE (EI)

EI Represents the formal or informal development of external organizational relationships that either receive subject matter expertise or produce communications of the organizational culture. Examples of this are:

> Joining Minority Chambers
> Gifting & Philanthropy
> Marketing Campaigns

Engaging in 1 or many of these project types is not D&I; further, stand-alone projects fail to meet the people management priorities of D&I over time. All empirical evidence of sentiment analysis on D&I and the statistical measures of inclusion equity and belonging suggest that this merely having ongoing projects at an organization has not created parity across the 27 Diversity Types.

2.3 TWENTY-SEVEN DIVERSITY TYPES

Per our previous mention the 27 Diversity Types are which are protected classes in one or more countries that recognize the ISO.

1. Gender
2. Racial
3. Age
4. Ethnicity
5. Religion
6. Language / Accents
7. LGBTQ
8. Geographic Location
9. Cognitive Abilities
10. Physical Abilities
11. Mental Health
12. Neurodiversity
13. Military Status
14. Citizenship
15. Behavior/Ethnodiversity
16. Personality/Thought-Style

17. Cultural Background
18. Family Upbringing
19. Social Roles
20. Education
21. Income
22. Socioeconomic Status
23. Marital Status
24. Parental Status
25. Criminal Background
26. Political Beliefs
27. Work Skills

Diversity is an odd word when it is applied to business processes, as it is a catch-all term that can mean everything or too many things, rendering it meaningless. In the year of this second edition of the DISM publication, 2023, there are more than 8,000,000,000 types of diversity on the planet earth. If we do enough digging into te personal data make-up of every individual, we will find uniqueness, but that is not what is meant by the blanket term Diversity from an organizational D&I standpoint.

These 27, are the types or classes of people that show up in legal dockets or human resources (HR) documents in regards to grievances with the organization. They can be internal or external to the organization, meaning personnel managed by HR or suppliers that engage the supplier diversity (SD) branch of an organization, which is typically controlled by the procurement functionality of the organization. These definitions below are both an example and a test. There are more than 27 represented in this text. While these types of people can have many or seemingly endless sub-categories, we'd like to know if you can tell which ones are redundant from a process design standpoint.

Note: these definitions are contextualized by institutions from the United States of America, as it has largest population individuals who identify outside of an established local normative and the largest number of identifiable organizations of any sovereign nation recognized by the ISO. We do hope that the referencing of American institutions is not offensive, and that readers will join us in scaling the national and hyper local reference points for what the 27 Diversity Types will become.

COGNITIVE DIFFERENT-ABILITIES

Cognitive "disabilities", also known as intellectual functioning, are recognized by the Equal Employment Opportunity Commission (EEOC) when an individual meets this criteria:

> - Intellectual functioning level (IQ) below 70-75
> - Significant limitations in adaptive skills — the basic conceptual, social and practical skills needed for everyday life
> - Disability began before age 18

Different functioning may affect an individual's memory, problem-solving abilities, attention, communication, linguistics, as well as verbal, reading, math and visual comprehension. However, having an intellectual disability does not mean the person is not capable of great success as an employee.

Some of the most famous and successful people in the world have cognitive disabilities ranging from Dyslexia, ADHD and Dyspraxia. To name a few: Satoshi Tajiri, the creator and designer of Pokemon, has Asperger's Syndrome; Bill Gates, the founder of Microsoft, has Dyslexia; Emma Watson, famous actress and activist, has ADHD.

Intellectual functioning can be difficult to notice, understand and communicate for both employees and employers, so it's important to provide employees with a variety of tools and resources to can help them function optimally at their job. The Job Accommodation Network provides a list of possible accommodations employers can provide to support employees of all abilities.

PHYSICAL ABILITIES & DIFFERENT-ABILITIES

Hiring individuals with varying disabilities and experiences will not only help your team build a more diverse and inclusive environment, but bring unique perspectives and ideas to help your company reach a wider market of customers and clients.

Start by checking how your company stands against the national Disability Equality Index. Also, consider some of these simple ways to boost disability inclusivity at your office and throughout your hiring process:

> Establish an Employee Resource Group (ERG)
> Offer comprehensive health benefit packages
> Partner with disability advocacy groups
> Design your website and application process with accessibility in mind
> Create an internship program for people with disabilities

Additionally, ensure your office is ADA compliant and make available ramps, automated doors, visual aids, telephone headsets, screen readers as well as accommodations for service animals, so if a job seeker or employee requires an aid of some sort, you are prepared to support their needs.

MENTAL HEALTH

Employee wellness is becoming a major trend in the HR space, but too often mental health is left out of the conversation. Without the support and resources to seek and receive the help employees need, companies may see an increase in absenteeism, work-family conflict, increased mental health and behavioral problems and even higher turnover rates.

To combat the stigma around mental health in the workplace, employers are improving resources, like insurance benefits, to cover mental health services and build a more inclusive company culture that supports mental health.

NEURODIVERSITY

Neurodiversity, as defined by the National Symposium on Neurodiversity "is a concept where neurological differences are to be recognized and respected as any other human variation. These differences can include those labeled with Dyspraxia, Dyslexia, Attention Deficit Hyperactivity Disorder, Dyscalculia, Autistic Spectrum, Tourette Syndrome, and others."

While there may be certain stereotypes and stigmas around neurodiverse individuals, research has found that some conditions, like autism and dyslexia, enhance an individual's ability to recognize patterns, retain information and excel in math — all critical skills for any job.

BEHAVIOR & ETHODIVERSITY

Everyone has their own unique mannerisms and behavior patterns they develop throughout their lives. Such behaviors are a result of an individual's upbringing, family, friends, culture, etc., and they can be interpreted in different ways. This is an important element of diversity to recognize because while a behavior may seem ordinary or unremarkable to you, to someone else it may seem rude, odd or inappropriate.

For example, let's say you are on the elevator and your colleague doesn't start a conversation with you. That doesn't necessarily mean they are being rude, it may simply be uncomfortable or uncommon for them to converse in such close and brief quarters.

Behavioral diversity or ethodiversity can be highly specific and subtle between individuals. It's important to remember that behavior is a result of a person's unique experiences, and if something feels odd, rude or inappropriate, consider politely asking them about why they do what they do rather than reacting negatively or being judgmental.

PERSONALITY & THOUGHT-STYLE

Bringing a variety of different personalities and thought-styles into a workplace can bring both stressful situations and genius creativity. To avoid the former, companies opt for hiring for culture fit, which consequently halt's the latter. Instead, companies should hire for culture add in pursuit of diverse personalities that work well together and challenge one another's ideas and thoughts.

It's difficult to know a person's personality and thought-style by their resume or even interview, which is why 22% of companies ask job candidates, as well as employees, to complete personality tests. Doing so helps companies understand their strengths, weaknesses and gaps and build a company culture that supports extroverts, introverts and everyone in-between.

While a number of companies boast about their team's vast 'diversity of thought,' it shouldn't be the only metric by which your team is measuring its diversity. Know that by hiring individuals with a wide range of diverse traits listed in this article, you will naturally acquire people with diverse personalities and thought-styles.

CULTURAL BACKGROUND

There are a number of factors that make up different cultures, including traditional food, language, religion and customs. The United States alone has several different cultures within each region, state and even town.

While a lot of people enjoy learning about other cultures for short time periods, it's an entirely different experience to work with individuals on a daily-basis who come from different cultures.

Cultural differences can bring a wealth of learning opportunities as well as some complicated challenges and barriers among employees who are unfamiliar or uncomfortable with one another's unique cultures. For example, cheek kisses are fairly common in French culture, and if you have a colleague or candidate who practices such behavior, they may view a cheek kiss as a friendly hello, whereas you may find that quite inappropriate at work.

Above everything, it's important to educate your team about different cultures and celebrate the differences. Additionally, creating a culture that encourages open communication will help employees explore each other's cultural differences without creating a hostile work environment.

GEOGRAPHICAL LOCATION

Geographical location plays a major role in the culture, language, education, social roles, socioeconomic status, beliefs and ideologies with which a person is accustomed. Keep in mind that just because an individual lives in a particular location now, doesn't mean they've always lived there. It's important to get to know your candidates' and colleagues' rich history to better understand their unique experiences in life prior to working with you.

NATIONAL ORIGIN

No matter where your company is headquartered, how many remote employees your company has on staff or where you are physically located in the world, it is very likely that you will work and interact with people who were born in a different country than yourself.

Regardless of where a person may currently be located, the country where one is born within can provide a set of cultural traits that one may carry with them for their entire life. From religious beliefs to personal ethos and much more, a person's national origin can define many things about them that they may carry with them for life.

LANGUAGE, LINGUISTICS & ACCENTS

Reports from the United States Census Bureau found that at least 350 languages are spoken in the homes of Americans. Unlike most countries, and contrary to popular belief, the United States does not have an official language. However, language, linguistics and accents can play a significant role in an individual's ability to get and keep a job.

For job seekers, if a job description or recruitment materials are only in one language, like English, it may be difficult for them to apply for a role or make it through an interview process. While it is not feasible for any company to translate all of their recruitment materials into 350+ different languages, it can be helpful to provide a few additional translations for common languages in your community and workplace. You may also consider utilizing an online translation service or in-person interpreter for roles that don't require individuals to be fluent in a language to work.

Additionally, accents reflect the different ways individuals pronounce certain words within a language and such differences can lead to accent bias or perception, where people judge or discriminate against an individual's intelligence and abilities simply by the way they pronounce certain words. Individual's may also have an affinity for people who have a similar accent to their own. Understanding different accent biases will help you and your team to identify your own biases and challenge them when you meet people from different language backgrounds.

ETHNICITY

For starters, ethnicity is different from race, which we will cover in an upcoming section. Rather than biological factors, ethnicity is based on learned behaviors. Ethnicity is associated with culture, history, nationality, heritage, dress, customs, language, ancestry and geographical background. Common examples of ethnicity include: Hispanic or Latinx, Irish, Jewish, or Cambodian.

RACE

Unlike ethnicity, which we discussed earlier in this section, race is biologically determined. Examples of race include: White, Black or African American American, Indian or Alaska Native, Asian, Native Hawaiian or Other Pacific Islander.

Nadra Kareem Nittle provides a clear example of race versus ethnicity for Thought Co. stating that, "Race and ethnicity can overlap. For example, a Japanese-American would probably consider herself a member of the Japanese or Asian race, but, if she doesn't engage in any practices or customs of her ancestors, she might not identify with the ethnicity, instead considering herself an American.

CITIZENSHIP STATUS

In 1986, the Immigration Reform and Control Act (IRCA) was passed, making it illegal for employers to discriminate against candidates and employees when recruiting, referring, hiring or firing individuals based on their citizenship or immigration status. Even with such laws in place, citizenship status alone can play a significant role in foreign-born workers' ability to get a job or break past stereotypes related to immigrants and citizenship status.

In 2017, immigrants made up 13.6% of the U.S. population. Of those immigrants, 77% were lawful immigrants, 27% lawful permanent residents, 23% unauthorized immigrants and 5% were temporary lawful residents.

Gaining citizenship is certainly a challenging feat, and for those that do, the vast majority participate in the American workforce. In fact, foreign-born persons had a significantly lower unemployment rate at 3.5% in 2018, compared to native-born citizens at 4%.

AGE

At any given time, there are several generations employed in the workforce. Each generation has its own distinct differences defined by the time period people were born and the unique social, political and economic changes that occurred during their upbringing.

In the workforce, such differences can pose challenges for individuals among generations. These challenges can turn into an unconscious bias known as ageism. Ageism in the workplace is defined as the tendency to have negative feelings about another person based on their age.

Stereotypes of different generations contribute to this bias. For example, baby boomers are seen as workaholics, Generation Xers are risk takers, millennials care about meaningful work and now Generation Zers ghost employers and seek job security. Such stereotypes can lead employers and colleagues to believe there are skills gaps and life milestones (like having children or retiring) that may affect certain age groups from excelling at their company.

While ageism can affect any member of the workforce, 58% of workers notice age bias when people enter their 50s. On the other hand, people under 25 years old are 2x less likely to experience age discrimination.

FAMILY & UPBRINGING

Family has a significant impact on every individual's life. It plays a role in a person's upbringing and provides support throughout an individual's life. While some families are biologically related, others are chosen.

No matter what an individual's family situation is, as an employer, it's important to understand that everyone has obligations outside of work to the ones they love. Not only that but by providing perks and benefits such as family medical leave, flexible work hours, child and elder care benefits, you will help employees foster close relationships with their family, thus enhancing their work-life balance and satisfaction.

IDEOLOGIES

Ideologies are the conceptions an individual, group or culture have about different aspects of life. Most people have distinct economic, political and religious ideologies that are influenced by the people in their family, their upbringing, geographical location and education. Ideologies play a part in how often and comfortable employees share their opinions with colleagues. Vastly differing ideologies may make individuals more cautious to start a conversation with a coworker if they know it could lead to a heated debate.

MORALS

Morals reflect an individual's beliefs for acceptable thoughts and behaviors. Morals tend to reflect an individual's upbringing, family, life experiences, income, ideologies, cultural background, citizenship status, privilege, personalities, socioeconomic status, social roles, as well as social, religious, political and worldly beliefs.

Most companies seek individuals who share the same personal morals, values and ethics to align with the company's core values. For employers, shared morals can alter how a company prioritizes its work and the impact it makes on the industry, local community and the world at large.

SOCIAL ROLES

Social roles are constructs that are influenced by certain demographics of an individual, such as age, behavior, gender and culture. A common example is that of gender roles, which are assigned to individuals the moment their sex is identified and have unique precepts that vary by culture. Stereotypes are often correlated with social roles held about a particular demographic and can affect an individual's ability to move into certain professional roles, industries and face barriers, which is evident between men and women with the Glass Ceiling.

To become a true equal opportunity employer and support diversity and inclusion in the workplace, it's important to become acutely aware of social roles and stereotypes unique to your culture, community, industry and workplace. Your team can help to break down barriers and open opportunities for people regardless of perceived social roles by attracting a diverse employee base in your recruitment materials. This trucking company did just that when they launched a recruitment campaign about women truckers to attract more female candidates.

GENDER IDENTITY

Gender roles are social constructs that vary by different cultures and are assigned to individuals at birth based on their biological sex. Once a child is assigned their gender, they are more or less segregated into either the male or female gender binaries.

Rather than these distinct binaries, popular belief finds that there is a spectrum of gender identities that may or may not correspond to the individual's sex assigned at birth. A few common non-binary gender identities include: non-binary, transgender, gender-transition, gender queer, gender fluid and demigender, however there is a long list of other non-binary identities you should learn about. There are also ungender identities, such as agender, non-gendered, genderless and gender-free.

Such identities are defined by the individual and how they view and expect others to view themself. It's important to keep in mind that individuals may identify differently from how you perceive their identity, so it's courteous to ask for people's preferred pronouns as well as share your own.

GENDER EXPRESSION

Gender expression, which may be different from an individual's sex or gender identity, refers to the external appearance of an individual's gender identity. Gender expression may be interpreted through clothing, hair, makeup, voice, behavior, mannerisms, interests and preferred pronouns. Again, because you can not assume an individual's gender even based on their gender expression, it's important to ask for their preferred pronouns. For more information on how to become an inclusive workplace for all gender identities and expressions, check out the Human Rights Campaign's guide to gender identity & gender expression in the workplace.

SEX

Unlike gender identity and gender expression, sex refers to the biological and genetic differences between male and female bodies. More specifically, women are born with two X chromosomes and men are born with one X and one Y chromosome. Typically, once a child is assigned their gender based on biological sex, they are more-or-less segregated into either the male or female gender binaries.

However, contrary to popular belief, biology of sex, similar to gender, has a spectrum of differences that cannot be classified simply as man and woman. Some people who are born with a combination of sex characteristics and reproductive organs are classified on the genetic sex spectrum called intersex.

SEXUAL ORIENTATION

Sexual orientation is also different from gender identity, gender expression and biological sex. Sexual orientation is defined by the Human Rights Campaign as "an inherent or immutable enduring emotional, romantic or sexual attraction to other people." Common sexual orientations include heterosexual, gay, lesbian, bisexual, asexual, pansexual and questioning.

As of yet, less than half of U.S. states have laws in place that protect employees from discrimination based on sexual orientation and gender identity. That doesn't mean employers can't create a diverse and inclusive workplace by:

- Educating your team about different gender identity terms.
- Asking candidates and employees about their gender pronouns.
- Creating an Employee Resource Group to support the LGBTQIA+ individuals at your workplace.

EDUCATION

Education varies greatly by location, school and teacher, and can be heavily influenced by national, state and district laws and requirements. This means that no single individual will have the exact same education. Not only that, but high-level education can be extremely expensive and unattainable for a significant part of the American population, and for upper-level jobs (or even entry-level jobs) post-high school degrees are often required.

The Bureau of Labor Statistics found in 2015 that the correlation between the level of education and unemployment rate is quite startling.

diversity-in-the-workplace-education-bls.png

Image via bureau of labor statistics

The average cost of a four-year college degree continues to rise, leaving recent grads who took out loans to pursue their dreams with on average, $29,800 of debt as of 2018. Not surprisingly, many talented young professionals are looking for alternative career paths that don't require such exorbitant costs.

On the flip side, employers are creating opportunities to help such professionals bypass college in exchange for applicable experiences.

Some companies no longer require candidates to complete a Bachelor's or Master's degree to compete for a role. Instead, companies are focusing on experiences, as well as hard and soft skills to qualify candidates. Additionally, removing education requirements allows candidates with more diverse, non-traditional backgrounds to apply.

INCOME

Income plays a major role in every individual's life starting from the day they are born and throughout their upbringing, professional career and into retirement. Income can be affected by geographical location, taxes, family, education, skills and socioeconomic background. Unconscious biases related to an individual's age, gender, gender identity and expression, sexual orientation, race, ethnicity and privilege can also affect their income.

In 2019, the Paycheck Fairness Act (PFA), first devised in 1997, was passed. This act builds upon existing legislation with three key components:

> It prohibits employers from asking candidates how much they previously made.
> It allows employees to share their pay with work colleagues.
> It requires employers to disclose all pay information with the Equal Employment Opportunity Commission.

Other income-based laws you should know about include the the Equal Pay Act of 1963, which prohibits pay discrimination based on gender and the Lilly Ledbetter Fair Pay Act of 2009, which prohibits gender-based wage discrimination and allows workers to sue for discrimination. While these acts are certainly steps in the right direction, there is still work to be done. Just check out this graph below for discrepancies in pay based on gender, race and ethnicity in the United States in 2018.

SOCIOECONOMIC STATUS

Socioeconomic status (SES) is the measurement and categorization of people based on their education, income and occupation. It is also a strong indicator of privilege, as well as the opportunities and resources an individual has access to in order to excel at school and work.

Additionally, SES is found to contribute significantly to one's mental health, physical health, stress, performance and functioning both in the workplace and in life.

To support candidates and employees of all SES, it's important to consciously create and distribute recruitment content that will reach and resonate with individuals of varying SES. As an employer, make sure to provide adequate salaries, benefits and resources to help individuals who are impacted by their own SES.

LIFE EXPERIENCES

Life experiences encompass all of the unique work, education, military, private and public occurrences an individual undergoes throughout their life that contributes to who they are, how they view the world and how they interact with others.

PRIVILEGE

Privilege refers to social power that can be inhibited or compounded based on an individual's sex, gender identity, race, ethnicity, religion, age, citizenship status, socioeconomic status, social role, cultural background and disability status. Privilege can affect a person's ability to obtain certain levels and quality of education, jobs, higher income and opportunities throughout life.

For employers, it is important to consider an individual's privilege and the opportunities they may or may not have access to due to their personal demographics. Let's not forget the recent college admissions scandal, which is an excellent example of how privilege and opportunity — rather than merit — can provide some individuals with more highly regarded experiences than others.

MARITAL STATUS

Marriage is a major event for many people. Not only that, but getting married, divorced, separated or becoming widowed can alter an individual's beliefs, geographical location, income, parental status, family, citizenship status, socioeconomic status, privilege, family and even behaviors.

Similar to gender bias, marital status bias can prevent highly qualified individuals from getting a job or excelling in their career. And while there are national laws that prohibit employers from discriminating against an individual's gender, sex and sexual orientation, only some states have specific laws prohibiting marital status discrimination in the workplace.

Marital status can especially affect an individual in the workplace if their partner also works in the same place. Some companies have an anti-nepotism policy in place to prevent a family member from working on the same team or in hierarchy to one another.

PARENTAL STATUS

While parental status can affect both mothers and fathers, in particular, pregnant women, working mothers and women of childbearing age face a motherhood penalty or maternal wall. Stereotypes related to a woman's role and needing time off after childbirth and for childcare often place women at a disadvantage in their careers compared to men and fathers.

Not only that, but female candidates are more likely to be asked questions about their parental plans and responsibilities during an interview. Even though discriminating against parents and pregnant people is illegal, inquiring about a job seeker's parental status technically isn't illegal.

In addition to working mothers, 54% of women with a young child leave their job because they need to care for their child. For individuals who take a large chunk of time off to fulfill caregiving needs, it can be extremely difficult for them to explain the gaps in their resume and find employers willing to support them as they reenter their career.

Employers can support working parents by reducing unconscious bias against them and by providing benefits like flexible work hours, childcare benefits, parental leave and adoption assistance to ease the challenges that working parents face and keep top employees in its workforce.

MILITARY EXPERIENCE

Military veterans offer a wealth of skills, knowledge and experience, making them exceptional contributions to any role or company. However, many employers are unfamiliar with military culture, experiences or common military language, which may make it difficult for them to understand the value such individuals can bring to a company. There are a number of resources available to help employers better understand how military skills are relevant to a specific role, such as this military skills translator and this skills matcher.

CRIMINAL BACKGROUND

The unemployment rate for people ages 25-44 who have formerly been incarcerated is more than five times higher than the national average. These individuals are in their prime working age but are struggling to find a company that will hire them with a criminal background.

And while some states provide incentives by offering tax breaks for companies that hire candidates with felony convictions, other states allow employers to require criminal history on job applications, perpetuating issues of social bias. In recent years, politicians from both sides have made efforts to support incarcerated individuals, from Obama's Fair Chance Business Pledge (2016) to Trump's First Step Act (2018). Today, however, it's still up to employers to decide whether or not they will allow an individual's past to prevent them from excelling in a rewarding career in the future.

POLITICAL BELIEFS

There are a lot of different opinions on how, when and if politics should be allowed in the workplace. For some, such discussions are a great way to connect with and engage in stimulating conversations unrelated to work. However, when colleagues have radically different political affiliations and views, controversy can erupt, making the workplace uncomfortable at best and unbearable at worst.

Not only that, but bringing politics into the workplace can lead to issues around political affiliation discrimination. And while there is no national law that prohibits employers from discriminating against a candidate or employee based on their political affiliation, a few states do.

All that being said, it can be extremely difficult to eliminate all traces of politics from the workplace. A lot can and is assumed about an individual's political affiliation based on their resume and personal interests. But is eliminating all politics really the answer? Just like every other element of diversity on this list, political diversity is also important for providing unique ideas, morals and beliefs to the workplace and fostering a truly diverse and inclusive workplace.

RELIGIOUS & SPIRITUAL BELIEFS

Whether or not people discuss their religious affiliations at work, it's important to create a workplace that is understanding and accepting of everyone's beliefs, even if they are different from one another.

Employers can do this by offering floating holidays so that employees can take time off for religious holidays and celebrations when they need. It's also important to respect individuals who wear religious clothing at work and ensure they are treated fairly and equally by their cohorts. Depending on your office and building layout, consider creating a space for private religious and spiritual practice so employees have a space to go during the day, and don't have to leave work or disrupt colleagues.

UNION AFFILIATION

A form of both organizational and functional diversity in the workplace, union affiliation can be a hot topic in many workplaces. Employees of an organization may either choose to or may be required to join a local union based on the rules of a collective bargaining agreement between the employer and the union, dependent on if their state has a "Right-to-Work" law that prohibits labor unions and employers from entering into contracts in which only unionized employees may be hired.

Labor union membership is intended as a way to protect employees from rights violations in their workplace, such as discrimination, overtime without pay, retaliation, privacy and whistleblower rights, however, many employees may be opposed to joining a labor union for a variety of reasons. Regardless of union status, all employees are still responsible for fulfilling their individual job requirements.

WORK EXPERIENCES

There's no doubt that every single workplace is different. Every company has their own unique mission, core values, policies, culture and benefits, which vary by region, industry, size and employer. Each time an employee moves into a new role, industry or company, they bring their previous work experiences and skills with them.

For employers, it's often beneficial to attract talent with diverse work experience, even hiring out-of-market candidates. Such experiences can help your team better understand different aspects of your own industries or reach new customer markets, so don't count candidates out just because they have different workplace experiences.

SKILLS

Skill set is a less obvious type of diversity, but one that is hugely important to the recruitment process. Depending on their professional history, candidates will have a particular skill set. However, based on their personal experiences and background, they'll have a vastly different set of strengths that can benefit your business and culture. Suss out individual skills — emotional intelligence, budding leadership abilities and the like — to create a positive culture that allows employees to excel.

While some skills are innate, others are learned. In the workplace, we tend to focus on the skills that directly apply to one's specific role. However, there are a number of other skills an individual picks up on through their personal interests and experiences that make them excellent at their job. If you are able to hone in on these unique skills and encourage employees to bring them to work, your team will surely excel in innovation and creativity.

SENIORITY

Workplaces change over time, however, many employees will remain with a company for several years and gain seniority as their roles develop and new employees are welcomed into the workplace. Different levels of seniority at a company may lead to varying sets of opinions or values about how the company operates and may also be influenced by factors like age and personal beliefs. Some newer employees may carry a sense of inferiority to a senior employee, or may be asked to report to senior employees in some cases, however, all employees within an organization are guaranteed the same rights and are expected to complete the duties within their job description.

MANAGEMENT STATUS

Similar to seniority, management status is a form of organizational diversity that is present in nearly every workplace. The vast majority of employees at every organization has somebody to report to and has a say in how their day-to-day time is spent at a company, as well as a set of expectations for the reportee to adhere to. Organizational hierarchy is put in place to ensure that an organization is able to function appropriately and scale over time. Employees of varying management styles may have different sets of expectations applied to them but all employees are guaranteed the same rights while performing their duties.

JOB FUNCTION/DEPARTMENT

Regardless of management status or seniority, job function and departmental placement are forms of organizational diversity that affect how people perform in the workplace. Different jobs place different expectations on people, meaning that experiences between employees of the same workplace, as well as the backgrounds that have brought them into the same workplace, will vary greatly.

2.4 THIRTY-TWO DOMAINS OF DIVERSITY AND INCLUSION

Developing an inclusive workplace requires an ongoing commitment to Diversity and Inclusion (D&I) to address inequalities in organizational systems, policies, processes, and practices as well as people's conscious and unconscious biases and behaviors.

This international standard provides guidelines to organizations on diversity and inclusion, D&I principles, practices, approaches, methods, and mechanisms, to enable and support equity, fairness, equality, and accessibility in workplace contexts. It recognizes that each organization is different and that decision-makers need to determine the most appropriate approach to integrate D&I into the organization's business processes, based on the organization's context. It can also foster consistency and fairness in the management and development of people in the supply chain, the delivery of the organization's products and services, and the interaction with other stakeholders.

The standard includes guidance and methods, and is structured to:

    a. Present a set of Principles that demonstrate ongoing commitment to valuing diversity and inclusion (D&I) that should be fostered by governing bodies and leaders.

b. Provide guidance on D&I Roles and Responsibilities, which includes a Framework, Outcomes, Actions, and Measures to foster development of an inclusive workplace.

DIVERSITY & INCLUSION GUIDANCE AND METHODS

c. Identify Roles and Responsibilities that would be accountable for achieving the potential D&I outcomes.
d. Identify Outcomes of leveraging diversity through inclusiveness, such as increased workforce engagement, creativity, innovation, productivity, and retention.
e. Identify diversity and inclusion (D&I) Actions (using a plan-do-check-act approach), which can lead to the desired outcomes.
f. Identify Measures for assessing effectiveness of the D&I Actions to address D&I risks, opportunities, impacts and outcomes.

2.5 ISO REFERENCES AND DEFINITIONS

ISO-30415:2021

This International Standard provides guidance on diversity and inclusion for organizations, including their governance bodies, leaders, workforce and their recognized representatives, and other stakeholders. It is intended to be scalable to the needs of all types of organizations in different sectors, whether in public, private, government or non-governmental organizations (NGO), regardless of size, type, activity, industry or sector, growth phase, or country-specific requirements.

This international standard identifies a set of principles, roles and responsibilities, actions, policies, processes, practices, and measures to evaluate impacts and outcomes to enable and support effective diversity and inclusion in the workplace. It recognizes that each organization is different and that decision-makers need to determine the most appropriate approach according to their organization's context.

This International Standard is voluntary and does not address the specific aspects of relations with labour unions, work councils, country-specific compliance or legal requirements or litigation.

DEFINITIONS AND NORMATIVE REFERENCES

The following pages are referred to in the text in such a way that references the ISO 30400, Human Resource Management (HRM) — Vocabulary. D&I is not HRM but it has stemmed from our collective examination of HRM over the past decades.

TERMS AND DEFINITIONS

For the purposes of this text, the terms and definitions given in ISO 30400 and the following apply.

ISO and IEC maintain terminological databases for use in standardization at the following addresses:

> ISO Online browsing platform: available at http: //www .iso .org/obp
> IEC Electropedia: available at http: //www .electropedia .org/

For the purposes of this document, the terms and definitions given in ISO 30400 Vocabulary, ISO 30408 Guidelines on Human Governance, ISO 30405 Guidelines on Recruitment, and ISO 10667 Assessment service delivery -- Procedures and methods to assess people in work and organizational settings, and the following apply.

accessibility extent to which facilities, work environments, systems, services, and products can be used by the broadest range of people (modified: ISO 27500 2011 2.3)

> Note 1 to entry: The concept of accessibility addresses the full range of user capabilities and is not limited to users with a disability; the aim is to achieve high levels of effectiveness, efficiency and user satisfaction whilst paying attention to the full

range of capabilities and universal design principles (modified: ISO 9241-20 2018 3.1).

accommodation reasonable adjustments process by which a person or organization adjusts to new circumstances.

> Note 1 to entry: Organizational policies on making reasonable adjustments to accommodate people with disabilities to access the same opportunities and services as non-disabled people, and to ensure that people with different abilities can contribute to their full potential.

> Note 2 to entry: Adjustments may vary according to individual circumstances but must be effective and practical. Examples include making adjustments to premises, modifying equipment, ensuring information is available in an accessible format, direct or supported use of assistive technologies, altering working hours or duties, and allowing absence for treatment and rehabilitation.

> Note 3 to entry: Through proactive support, organizations can enhance employability for people of differing abilities by making accommodations and reasonable adjustments.

accountability State of being answerable for decisions and activities to the organizations governing body, legal authorities, and more broadly, its stakeholders (ISO 26000 2010 2.1)

> Note 1 to entry: Obligation of an organization and its people to account for their roles, responsibilities and actions, and for completion of a deliverable or task, and to disclose opportunities, risks and outcomes in a transparent manner.

benefits non-cash provisions provided within an organization's reward policies, processes and practices

> Note 1 to entry: Although pay and benefits are often referenced together, the intent to define benefits separately is to describe the broad range of non-pay elements that an organization can provide (for example, paid leave, healthcare, company cars, childcare vouchers, and free or subsidized meals).

> Note 2 to entry: Although they have a financial value and cost for organizations, for example paid leave, pensions and company cars,

they may be offered based on the desire to care for the workforce and organizational well-being and engagement.

› Note 3 to entry: Financial, legal and socio-economic factors influence the development and shaping of an organization's reward policies and practices.

diversity characteristics of differences and similarities between people

› Note 1 to entry: Dimensions of diversity are the demographic other personal characteristics of the workforce, often expressed statistically, for example, age, disability, sex, sexual orientation, gender, race, colour, nationality, ethnic or national origin, religion or belief.

› Note 2 to entry: Diversity includes factors that influence the identities and perspectives that people bring when interacting at work.

› Note 3 to entry: Diversity can support the development of workplace environments and practices that foster learning from others to gain diverse perspectives on inclusiveness

employee resource groups (ERG's) business resource groups (BRG's) people with shared demographic and other personal characteristics, or affinity with these characteristics, who join together to demonstrate commitment to diversity and promote inclusion in the workplace

› Note 1 to entry: Examples of personal characteristics can include age, disability, sex, sexual orientation, gender, race, colour, nationality, ethnic or national origin, religion or belief.

› Note 2 to entry: These groups can raise awareness, lead, and provide support for D&I strategic objectives and actions.

› Note 3 to entry: Feedback from these groups can inform an organization's vision, mission and D&I strategy related to workforce development, retention and engagement, which can also foster a sense of belonging.

› Note 4 to entry: Ideally, these groups are sponsored by organizational leaders and usually have a written terms of reference and an allocated budget.

equality equal treatment and opportunities to participate and contribute

> Note 1 to entry: People should not be treated less favourably because of their demographic and other personal characteristics.

> Note 2 to entry: It includes equal treatment, or in some instances, treatment that is different but equivalent in terms of rights, benefits, obligations and opportunities. (ISO 26000 2010 2.8)

equity principle that people should be subject to policies, processes and practices that are fair, as far as possible, and free from bias (modified ISO 10667 2011 2.13)

fairness impartial, equitable and respectful treatment or behaviour that strives to alleviate favouritism or discrimination

> Note 1 to entry: Organizational policies, processes and practices that are fair and impartially applied support the development and maintenance of an inclusive workplace.

inclusion process of including all stakeholders in organizational contexts

> Note 1 to entry: Organizational policies, processes and practices that are fair and impartially applied can support an inclusive workplace.

> Note 2 to entry: This involves the entire workforce having access to opportunities and resources to enable their contribution to the organization.

> Note 3 to entry: entry: This involves stakeholders from different groups being accepted, welcomed, enabled to have a voice, and to develop a sense of belonging.

Inclusive culture values, beliefs and practices that influence the conduct and behaviour of people and organizations, and that include and value the perspectives and contributions of diverse stakeholder.

inclusiveness process of aiming at achieving inclusion

- Note 1 to entry: An organization is realizing inclusiveness when it seeks to foster and value the perspectives and contributions of every stakeholder.
- Note 2 to entry: Inclusivity is demonstrated when an organization strives to include many different types of stakeholders and treat them fairly and equally.

intersectionality combination of one or more demographic and personal characteristics that are part of a person's identity

- Note 1 to entry: These personal characteristics include age, disability, sex, sexual orientation, gender, race, colour, nationality, ethnic or national origin, religion or belief, as well as characteristics related to socio-economic context.
- Note 2 to entry: These personal and socio-economic characteristics intersect, such that each characteristic is linked to other characteristics, and influence a person's life and work experiences.

learning and development broad, multifaceted set of activities focused on improving the performance of the organization and the knowledge, skills and abilities of its people

- Note 1 to entry: It includes a variety of approaches and methods, such as induction, on-the-job or off-the-job training, coaching, mentoring, and forms of self-development aimed at helping people develop knowledge, skills, abilities and behaviours related to their job, employability, and well-being, in addition to meeting the organization's strategic objectives.
- Note 2 to entry: Learning is the act of obtaining or acquiring new knowledge, skills, and abilities, and occurs through the impact of education, training, instruction, practices or study on the individual.
- Note 3 to entry: People also learn from others, which can raise awareness of the organization's diversity and inclusion principles and strategic objectives.
- 3.15 onboarding boarding induction processes of welcoming people into the organization, its culture, expectations, policies, people and their roles

stakeholder interested parties person or organization that can affect, be affected by, or perceive itself to be affected by a decision or activity.

supplier diversity deliberate approach to engage and support diverse suppliers, and to foster diversity and inclusion in the organization's supply chain

> Note 1 to entry: Supplier diversity processes could be integrated into supplier selection activities, contracting processes and objectives, such as, leveraging the demographics of the organization's customer base.

> Note 2 to entry: supplier diversity can be part of the organizational strategy, integrated with other organizational policies, processes, and practices, and linked to annual performance objectives cross-functionally.

Voice way an organization's people communicate their views and influence matters that affect them at work

> Note 1 to entry: The means by which people communicate views on employment and organizational issues, for instance through line managers, which can enable participation and involvement of people in influencing organizational decision-making.

> Note 2 to entry: Formal and informal mechanisms can be supported by workforce and organizational engagement and opinion surveys, face-to-face focus groups, Employee Resource Groups (ERGs), forums, social media platforms, and others.

> Note 3 to entry: Can be evident through discussions, consultations, negotiations and joint actions involving representatives of the organization and its workforce in social dialogue; this can be facilitated by labor unions, work councils, or workforce representatives present in the workplace.

working time period of activity, or working hours, defined by the daily start and finish times (ISO 2631-2 2003 3.3)

> Note 1 to entry: Period of time, during which people are carrying out activities and duties they have agreed to undertake.

> Note 2 to entry: It includes agreed minimum conditions, such as rest and leave entitlements, and opportunities for flexible or smart working. (BSI PAS 3000 Smart working)

> Note 3 to entry: It takes into account the changing nature of work and acknowledges issues that people face in the workplace, such as those with caring responsibilities.

PRINCIPLES

The following principles, taken together, are fundamental to these guidelines and, when applied, demonstrate commitment to valuing diversity and inclusion:

Human Capital. Valuing people in organizations and recognizing their intrinsic value, individually and collectively, in addition to any protections under the law, regulation and/or organizational protocol. [Ref: TC260 30414 HCR]

Governance. Exemplifying and promoting commitment to D&I through use of organizational governance systems policies, processes, practices, and operations. Application of effective governance includes ethics and ethical leadership, integrity, transparency, fairness, equity, equality, harassment and retaliation prevention, due process, assessment and evaluation, reporting, and independent validation (where appropriate).

Accountability for actions. For the organization, accountability to act in a socially responsible manner that is sustainable for itself, its communities, and societies. For members of the workforce, accountability to act in a manner that is respectful and inclusive.

Integration. Aligning D&I with organizational, financial, and human resource management outcomes and impacts.

Work. Creating an accessible and respectful workplace environment to foster inclusion and a sense of belonging that enables people to participate and bring their whole selves to work. When the composition of the workforce is representative of the community in which the organization operates, the benefits of diversity can be realized by all stakeholders.

Intersectionality. Recognizing and appreciating different dimensions of diversity in the workplace and how they interconnect and interrelate. This includes a variety of demographic and other personal characteristics, the inter-relationship of these.

Communication. To encourage civil discourse, respectful dialogue and behaviour between members of the workforce and other stakeholders, organizational communication should be accessible, multidirectional, and use explicit and implicit inclusive language, images and symbols, a variety of approaches, methods, and mediums that recognize the different abilities of people to access, understand and respond to communications in different ways.

Advocacy. To recognize, champion and value D&I, and to influence and promote inclusive organizational practice across the organisation and relationships with customers/clients, suppliers, communities, and other stakeholders

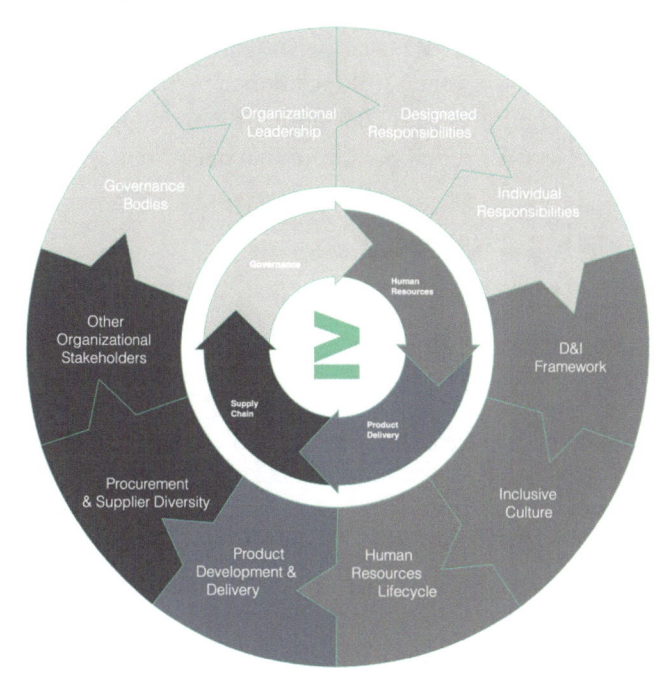

2.6 GOVERNANCE

D&I ROLES AND RESPONSIBILITIES

Everyone in the organization has a role and responsibility in the realization of the D&I principles, and in establishing and maintaining an inclusive culture at work. Inclusive behaviours ensure that ideas and contributions of stakeholders are welcomed and respected. Encouraging feedback from the workforce and other stakeholders can be used to effectively develop and communicate the importance of D&I as an organizational strategy, and to influence organizational outcomes and impacts throughout the entire organisational life cycle and in critical periods of change.

The organization's governance bodies and senior leadership teams' commitment to and accountability for D&I is demonstrated by ensuring that adequate resources and funding of D&I initiatives and activities is available. D&I responsibility should be designated to people with expertise and understanding of D&I. People who have designated responsibilities for D&I, people management, and stakeholder relationships are accountable for planning, implementing and monitoring policies, processes, and practices, and reviewing their effectiveness in achieving D&I strategic objectives. This includes recognizing the value of its relationships with customers/clients, suppliers and communities, and considering the outcomes and impacts of D&I strategic objectives across organizational operations.

GOVERNANCE BODIES

To ensure that D&I principles and strategic objectives are aligned with the vision, mission, strategy, systems, an organization's governance body has responsibility for:

> ❯ Have you determined senior leadership accountability for establishing D&I principles and strategic objectives, including the provision of resources to achieve them, and embedding D&I principles into the organizational culture?

- Are you demonstrating and role modelling behaviours that are required by the D&I principles, shared values and beliefs?
- Are you challenging behaviour that is inconsistent with D&I principles and ensuring that people who challenge inappropriate behaviour, and those who are affected by it, are protected and supported?
- Are you evaluating the organization's D&I risks and opportunities and progress in meeting its D&I strategic objectives?

ORGANIZATIONAL LEADERSHIP

Organizational leaders, as advocates and champions of D&I, have responsibility for:

- Are you establishing D&I principles and strategic objectives?
- Are you allocating resources to achieve D&I objectives, including sponsorship of initiatives, Employee Resource Groups (ERGs) and diversity councils where these exist, and others. This includes allocation of adequate time and support for participating and contributing to the achievement of D&I strategic objectives?
- Are you facilitating a positive organizational culture by establishing D&I expectations and accountability, communicating these to all stakeholders, and fostering inclusive relationships and shared values with an increasingly diverse workforce, consumer base, and supply chains?
- Are you clarifying and role modelling appropriate behaviour; clarifying, challenging and addressing inappropriate behaviour; and recognizing and rewarding D&I inclusive practices and behaviours?
- Are you directing that systems, policies, processes, and practices meet the D&I principles and strategic objectives, taking into account challenges, constraints, risks and opportunities?
- Are you considering demographic data, including the implications of intersectionality, when planning, designing, delivering, measuring and assessing the impact of their products and services on diverse markets and customers?
- Are you leading the organization's annual reporting process to ensure that D&I strategic objectives, risks and opportunities are discussed in a clear narrative description that is supported by robust evidence?

DESIGNATED RESPONSIBILITIES FOR D&I, PEOPLE MANAGEMENT, AND STAKEHOLDER RELATIONSHIPS

People with designated responsibility and accountability for D&I, people management, organizational culture, and stakeholder relationships have responsibility for:

> - Are you ensuring that D&I principles related to fairness, equity, equality, and transparency are integrated into systems, plans, policies, procedures and processes?
> - Are you sharing D&I knowledge, skills and expertise, and providing advocacy and guidance on policies, processes, and practices that promote diverse and inclusive organizational culture?
> - Are you demonstrating and role modelling appropriate behaviours, including in training, coaching and mentoring activities?
> - Are you directing, leading, sourcing, implementing, measuring and communicating the achievement of D&I objectives, outcomes and impact?
> - Are you ensuring that adequate resources are deployed to respond to opportunities, risks, constraints and challenges in order to achieve D&I strategic objectives?
> - Are you fostering an inclusive and diverse workplace by enabling access and adjustments to increase participation of underrepresented groups?
> - Are you ensuring policies, processes, practices and decisions about people, as they transition into, through, and out of the organization, are evidence-based and supported by checks and balances to mitigate the effects of bias?
> - Are you promoting the organization's D&I principles and strategic objectives through contracting arrangements with the supply chain, relationships with consumers and communities, and other external stakeholders?
> - Are you facilitating open channels of communication so that diverse perspectives are received with respect and without prejudice?

- Are you enabling a safe environment for D&I issues to be raised (including whistle blowing) and to ensure due process is applied for all stakeholders?
- Are you ensuring that stakeholder feedback is considered when monitoring the implementation of policies, processes, and practices to identify D&I impacts, outcomes, challenges, constraints and trends?
- Are you identifying the criteria and associated measures for D&I that are material to the organization?
- Are you evaluating the impact of policies, processes, and practices on (i) the development of an inclusive workplace (including the transition of people into, through, and out of the organization) and (ii) other stakeholders?
- Are you reviewing and reporting the status and progress against identified D&I strategic objectives (including the assessment of risk and opportunities), any recommendations for change, and inclusion in the organization's annual report?

INDIVIDUAL RESPONSIBILITIES INCLUDE:

- Is your team treating colleagues, customers, suppliers and other stakeholders with respect and fairness?
- Does your team meet expectations of the D&I principles and strategic objectives?
- Does your team demonstrate inclusive behaviour?
- Does your team challenge inappropriate behaviour (including whistle blowing)?
- Does your team actively foster inclusion, trust and a sense of belonging?

***Actions & Measures** are the elements of the ISO-30415 standard that are executed by the D&I Professionals (DIPs) focused on a specific organization. Actions are elements that DIPs execute and Measures are tolls or tactics that DIPs use to quantify their actions.*

2.7 DIVERSITY AND INCLUSION (D&I) FRAMEWORK

The D&I Framework and the human resource management life cycle policies, processes and practices, relating to attracting, developing and retaining a diverse workforce, should support the organization's vision and mission, align with D&I principles and strategic objectives, and influence D&I practices within the supply chain. Adopting a continuous improvement approach should include a cycle of planning, doing, checking and reviewing to support the identification of D&I risks and opportunities and the activities, review measures, and accountabilities required to achieve desired outcomes.

OUTCOMES

Individual, department, and group D&I objectives are aligned with the organization's vision, mission, strategy, and systems. Organizational leaders demonstrate commitment to D&I, and responsibilities and accountabilities are clearly defined. Strategic risks and opportunities are identified; implementation priorities are articulated, actioned and monitored. Organizational leaders, the workforce and other stakeholders, are aware of organizational expectations, participate in implementing D&I activities, and support the achievement of D&I objectives. Policies and practices are fair and equitable, representing the respective needs of the broadest range of people and other organizational stakeholders. The organization's workforce is representative of the community it operates in and serves. Evidence of progress in achieving D&I objectives is communicated to the workforce and other stakeholders on a recurring basis (e.g., in an annual review of performance). The D&I strategy is successfully implemented and results in positive outcomes for the organization, its workforce and other stakeholders.

ACTIONS

To achieve D&I strategic objectives pertaining to the D&I Framework, organizations should:

> Does your team ensure that D&I principles and strategic objectives are integrated into organizational policies, processes, and practices?

> Does your team regularly assess the relevance and alignment of D&I objectives against the organization's vision, mission, strategy, and systems, its external operating environment, and organizational culture in anticipation of change?

> Does your team ensure that all members of the workforce understand and share in the achievement of D&I objectives?

> Does your team ensure people, groups and departments objectives are aligned with D&I strategic objectives and that risks and opportunities are explored. Planning and implementation challenges and constraints should be documented, monitored and measured to support the evaluation of progress against D&I strategic objectives?

> Does your team review their plans, systems, underlying technologies, policies, processes, and practices; and ensure they are fair and equitable and do not cause adverse impact on people, groups or other stakeholders?

> Does your team consider D&I impacts and outcomes in procurement of goods and services, delivery of the organization's goods and services, and interactions with other stakeholders?

MEASURES

Organizations should use valid and reliable quantitative and qualitative measures to assess D&I risks and opportunities and the impact and outcomes of their D&I activities. Existing measures should be reviewed to see if they are relevant to supporting the evaluation of progress against D&I objectives in context with the organization's operating environment. Measures of workforce and other stakeholder perceptions of the organization's commitment to D&I can be drawn from focus groups, surveys, interviews and external review findings. Analysis of findings and data should support the identification and assessment of potential adverse effects of the organization's policies and practices on different groups, people or stakeholders.

Examples of D&I relevant measures include:

> Can you identify percentage changes of D&I risks and opportunities?
> Can you measure effectiveness of the activities in achieving D&I objectives against baseline data, resource allocation and identified challenges and constraints?
> Can you identify effectiveness of organizational involvement with stakeholders in relation to D&I?
> Can you identify the impact of leadership commitment to D&I on workforce and stakeholder awareness of D&I activities and objectives?
> Can you identify accessibility of information and effectiveness of communication methods and mediums?
> Can you identify trends in solicited and unsolicited feedback on D&I activities and objectives?
> Can you identify the percentage of the workforce that feel valued by the organization?
> Is there a record of the number of reported D&I incidents (e.g., complaints, grievances,)?

2.8 INCLUSIVE CULTURE

Inclusive organizational culture is determined by the vision, mission, and strategy set by governance and leadership, and is predominantly influenced by leaders and their approach to developing a diverse and inclusive organization. It is also influenced by principles, values, beliefs, behaviours, and expression of the lived experience of the people working for, or on behalf of, the organization. An inclusive organization enables fair and equitable access to jobs, careers, learning and development opportunities, and, through its relations with employees and other stakeholders, fosters a sense of connectedness and mutual respect. This is reinforced through the organisation's policies, processes and practices, for example in job design and hiring, to attract people with similar or diverse values, beliefs, knowledge, skills, abilities, and cognitive approaches.

OUTCOMES

Culture is aligned with the organization's vision, mission, D&I principles and strategic objectives. Leadership commitment to D&I is demonstrated in behaviours that foster trust and challenge bias, and an inclusive culture at work is promoted. The organization has a reputation for its diversity and inclusion initiatives and is externally recognized as an inclusive employer and preferred place to work, where all members of the workforce are encouraged to achieve their full potential. Collaboration and knowledge-sharing is valued as a norm. People have a voice, dialogue is encouraged, and diverse perspectives are respected and welcomed. The intersectionality of personal and socio-economic characteristics are recognised and supported, and people have a sense of belonging. People are welcomed to contribute, participate, and manage their work in a variety of ways. Improved organizational engagement is reflected in the way people value and respect each other and the organization's assets. Problem- solving and decision-making, creativity and innovation are improved through diverse groups working collaboratively. A safe work environment is realized and incidences of complaints, grievances and risks are recognized and reduced. Relationships with other stakeholders are enhanced and, consequently, service provision is enhanced.

ACTIONS

To achieve D&I strategic objectives for inclusive culture, organizations should:

> Does your team prioritize D&I principles, including the ethical considerations related to collecting and using individual demographic profile data, to support achievement of D&I strategic objectives, and to create, foster and promote an inclusive organizational culture through communications, outreach activities, and relationships with all stakeholders?

› Does your team enable people to share their demographic profile data, perspectives, voice their opinions, share concerns and make suggestions for change related to D&I through a variety of different mechanisms that foster dialogue and debate (such as focus groups, surveys, suggestions schemes and other stakeholder feedback methods)?

› Does your team communicate behavioural expectations that promote the importance of inclusive, respectful behaviour and prevention of harassment, micro-aggression, and any form of retaliation?

› Does your team establish feedback mechanisms to gain insight on the impacts of negative and positive behaviours on D&I strategic objectives, particularly when displayed by leaders; and data should be reviewed to ascertain the organization's D&I reputation as an inclusive organization?

› Does your team seek feedback on the culture at work from individuals, voluntary task groups, such as Employee Resource Groups (ERG's), committees, focus groups, workforce representatives, work councils, and labour union representatives, where they exist?

› Does your team collect data on health, safety and well-being (including absence), turnover and retention, and workplace conflicts to identify adverse impacts on demographic groups and their intersections.?

› Does your team report on the development of an inclusive organizational culture, workforce composition, D&I risks and opportunities, and action plans?

MEASURES

Examples of relevant D&I measures include:

› Can you analyze the effectiveness of D&I communications to determine which methods, format and channel have the most impact and provide insightful feedback?

› Can you analyze the effectiveness of outreach activities with stakeholders to ascertain awareness of D&I principles and strategic objectives?

- Can you analyze the frequency and number of learning and development activities that promote the importance of inclusive and respectful behaviour, the percentage of the workforce participating, and the impact of this learning and development on workforce behaviours?
- Can you analyze the percentage of the workforce that state that they feel valued by the organization in surveys and other feedback, including the percentage of the workforce that has shared their personal demographic data?
- Can you analyze findings of reported incidents, grievances, complaints, and disputes to identify D&I dimensions, and whether there are any disproportionate and/or adverse impacts related to implementation of the organization's systems, policies, processes and practices on individuals or groups in the organization and other stakeholders?
- Can you analyze reported sickness and other absence and retention and turnover data to identify D&I dimensions, and whether there are any disproportionate and/or adverse impacts related to implementation of the organization's systems, policies, processes and practices on individuals or groups in the organization?
- Can you analyze trends in solicited and unsolicited feedback, including engagement and satisfaction surveys, focus groups and interviews, learning and development feedback and assessments, and from messages of appreciation, awards and recognition related to D&I, to ascertain the organization's standing as an inclusive organization and any D&I impacts?
- Can you analyze changes in the demographic composition of the organization's governance bodies and workforce, and changes in the number and levels of D&I risks identified, including those relating to the health, safety and wellbeing of the workforce and other stakeholders?

2.9 HUMAN RESOURCES MANAGEMENT LIFECYCLE (HRMLC)

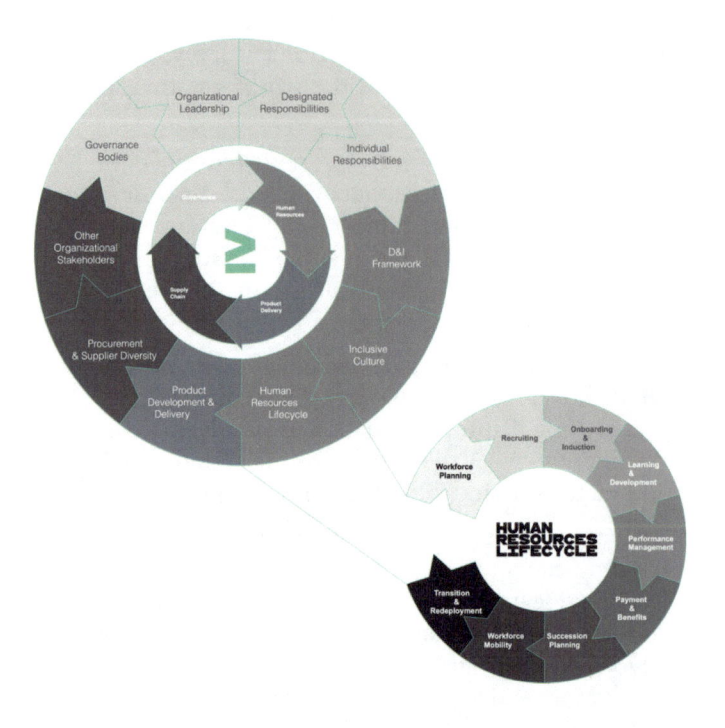

A principled approach to human resource management should be founded on trust, fairness, respect and transparency, and foster inclusion and a sense of belonging. There are D&I imperatives and implications in the Human Resource Management Life Cycle. This involves policies, processes and practices for identifying the organization's life cycle stage and the knowledge, skills and abilities required, and for attracting, developing, retaining, and outplacing people.

Adopting a continuous improvement approach should include a cycle of planning, doing, checking and reviewing to support the identification of D&I risks and opportunities in the following areas:

- Workforce planning
- Recruitment
- Onboarding and integration
- Learning and development
- Performance management
- Pay and benefits
- Succession planning
- Global workforce mobility
- Transition, redeployment, retirement and cessation of employment

WORKFORCE PLANNING

Workforce planning identifies current, transitional and future workforce demand and supply, in the context of the organization's life cycle stage: growth, no change, decline, restructure, amalgamations and closure. Workforce segmentation is a fundamental aspect in workforce planning, and there are two basic approaches: role-based segmentation, where jobs are segmented by value or type of work performed; and employee-based segmentation, where jobs are segmented by demographic, location or other observable or inferred characteristics. Workforce planning makes explicit the human resource requirements and enables the organization to anticipate and respond to identified D&I risks and opportunities, which includes using appropriate demographic data, metrics and other organisational key performance indicators.

Outcomes

Organizational D&I risks and opportunities are identified, addressed and monitored effectively in the organization's workforce plan. The organization's D&I framework is referenced in the workforce plan. D&I objectives in human capital requirements, including expertise building in key functions, is planned. Progress against D&I strategic objectives and employee-based segmentation priorities is evident. The organization is able to demonstrate that it is a diverse and inclusive organization.

Actions

To achieve D&I strategic objectives for workforce planning, organizations should:

> Does your team identify D&I implications of organizational strategies, including any potential disproportionate impact on various workforce segments in all levels?

> Does your team ensure the organization's workforce plan, including job roles, acknowledges intersectionality; identifies gaps in underrepresented groups (including knowledge, skills, abilities, attitudes and other factors required by the organization); and examines where knowledge, skills, abilities, attitudes and other factors required by the organization exist and where there are gaps or underrepresentation?

> Does your team identify job segments of the organization based on existing workforce segmentation and D&I dimensions; and the opportunities for inclusion should be assessed?

> Does your team identify and report on available supply and demand data and associated information gaps (quantitative and qualitative) pertaining to the segmented workforce and its diversity?

> Does your team foster and leverage relationships, both internally and externally, that strengthen diversity, equity and inclusion (such as establishing relationships with community organizations and educational institutions)?

Measures

Examples of relevant D&I measures include:

> Can your team analyze and evaluating workforce planning strategies for potential disproportionate impact on D&I impacts and outcomes?

> Can your team track and monitoring inclusion opportunities (such as, diversity within workforce segments, progression of people from underrepresented groups, including any intersecting D&I dimensions, and the distribution of skills and roles) contained in the workforce plan, and their impacts and outcomes?

RECRUITMENT

Recruitment includes the acquisition and selection of a suitably diverse workforce, which can be achieved through various forms of employment including but not limited to: continuing appointments, return-to-work after injury and disease, temporary assignments, apprenticeships, internships, projects and task forces, and volunteer workforces, which can positively impact access to socio-economic opportunities.

Outcomes

There is evidence that recruitment and selection processes proactively provide opportunities for candidates from underrepresented groups. There is evidence that the organization is aware of consequences involving unintended biases in recruitment processes, such as candidate experience in attraction, assessment and selection, interviewing, and hiring. There is evidence that candidates value the organization's employer brand, as a workplace where everyone is heard and respected, and perceived as a fair and inclusive organization.

Actions

To achieve D&I strategic objectives for recruitment, organizations should:

- › Does your team consider the culture at work, industry sector, location, and workforce planning needs. Candidates from various cultural backgrounds should be accepted, welcomed, and offered work opportunities on the basis of their knowledge, skills, abilities, and other factors?
- › Does your team use internal and external job posting processes that are transparent, fair, and inclusive, which foster non-discriminatory practices?
- › Does your team strengthen the employer brand as an inclusive organization, when directly or indirectly communicating, advertising or promoting job activities or opportunities, recruitment marketing should consider D&I principles and strategic objectives?

› Does your team ensure job descriptions are based on the nature of work performed and skills required, and include consideration of flexibility, accessibility, accommodations or reasonable adjustments for specific individual needs?

› Does your team adopt recruitment processes (including selection and assessment methods) that foster fair treatment of candidates, without discrimination or bias. Selections should be made based on the requirements of the role and the candidate's ability to perform it?

› Does your team examine where and how positions are filled, and source a mix of candidates from diverse groups?

› Does your team identify and attract a pool of people with diverse knowledge, skills, abilities, values and cultural perspectives, and demographic characteristics?

Measures

Examples of relevant D&I measures include:

› Can your team measure the range and types of methods and tools used for recruitment should and then include D&I and be recorded and reported?

› Can your team measure the number of applicants from diverse backgrounds who respond to internal and external postings that should be tracked?

› Can your team measure the proportion of inquiries, applicants, and candidates from each D&I dimension at each stage of the recruitment process to the number of appointments that should be recorded and evaluated?

ONBOARDING AND INDUCTION

Onboarding and induction is the way people are welcomed into the organization and its culture. This includes introducing the organization's D&I principles, shared values and strategic objectives, people and their roles, and policies, processes and practices. It is a shared responsibility between people with designated responsibilities for D&I and hiring managers. The purpose is to help people become successful in their teams/roles, address their needs and requirements, and encourage inclusive behaviours.

Outcomes

Effective onboarding and induction results in people feeling welcomed, included and valued, with their needs and requirements recognized and accommodated. People are aware and understand the importance of the organization's D&I principles, shared values and strategic objectives, and commitment to achieving these is demonstrated through inclusive behaviour. People are aware of D&I policies, know where to go for help and support on harassment, discrimination, retaliation, and whistle blowing, and how to access other resources (such as processes for resolving D&I issues or complaints), including helplines, employee assistance provisions, and ERGs (if available). People's contribution to organisational success is evident.

Actions

To achieve D&I strategic objectives for onboarding and induction, organizations should:

> Does your team prioritize the importance of the D&I principles, align with the D&I strategic objectives, and communicate that everyone has a role and responsibility in making the organization inclusive by welcoming and respecting everyone's ideas and contributions?

> Does your team ensure structured onboarding process plans are implemented for the induction of new people into the organization from their first day, first week, and first three months. The onboarding process should ensure that diverse needs are met and individual requirements regarding work environment, facilities and technologies are recognize?

> Does your team ensure that diverse training needs are met, including orientation to the D&I principles and strategic objectives, specific individual learning and development and progression opportunities, incorporating coaching and mentoring for people in underrepresented groups?

> Does your team clarify behavioral expectations and include examples on inclusive and exclusive behavior?
> Does your team provide information on relevant D&I policies, processes, practices, and resources, including how to access helplines, employee assistance provisions, and ERGs (if available). This should also identify where and who to go to for help and support on resolving D&I issues or complaints?

Measures

Examples of relevant D&I measures within the first three months include:

> Can your team measure the number of D&I onboarding and induction activities provided, the number of people who complete them, and participant feedback on their effectiveness?
> Can your team measure the frequency of communications about D&I principles and strategic objectives, including relevant policies, processes and practices?
> Can your team assess the level of understanding about D&I principles and strategic objectives - Assess the level of awareness about policies, processes and practices?
> Can your team measure the number of accommodations and reasonable adjustments requested and satisfied?
> Can your team measure the number of coaching and mentoring opportunities offered to, and accepted by, people from underrepresented groups?
> Can your team measure the number of people accessing support systems and D&I trends identified?
> Can your team measure the number of people stating in surveys, or through other feedback methods, that they feel welcomed and included into the organization?

LEARNING AND DEVELOPMENT

Learning and Development is an approach to raising awareness of D&I principles and enhancing knowledge, skills and abilities to achieve D&I strategic objectives. By systematically providing learning and development opportunities in an equitable manner, the organization can enable an inclusive workplace, increase performance, strengthen participation, mitigate bias, and contribute to increased job satisfaction. Learning and development includes coaching and mentoring programs, which can enhance recruitment, improve performance, and reduce turnover. Coaching and mentoring helps people to develop their full potential and improve personal and professional performance.

Outcomes

Effective learning and development results in organizational and managerial awareness, and understanding of the importance of the organization's D&I principles, shared values and strategic objectives. D&I is a core concept integrated into all learning and development programs. Coaching and mentoring relationships are successful, and contribute to increased job satisfaction and improved organizational performance. People feel included, and develop and demonstrate inclusive behaviour.

Actions

To achieve D&I strategic objectives for learning and development, organizations should:

> **Does yo**ur team make learning and development available and accessible to all members of the workforce to allow everyone to contribute, participate and benefit from the learning, making reasonable adjustments or accommodations, as required?

> Does your team ensure that D&I is incorporated into learning and development processes so that resources are made available (such as funding streams, appropriately qualified professionals, accessible venues, and learning platforms)?

> Does your team build sensitivity, conviction, compassion, respectful behaviour and inclusiveness into session goals?

> Does your team design D&I learning and development activities to increase awareness, develop knowledge, skills, and abilities, mitigate bias and foster insight into the benefits of having a range of perspectives, abilities, values and beliefs?

- ❯ Does your team provide management development on D&I principles and inclusive leadership practices?
- ❯ Does your team ensure learning and development programs raise awareness of D&I principles, policies, processes and practices?
- ❯ Does your team integrate D&I concepts into general organizational learning and development programs so that D&I is not viewed as a stand-alone concept?
- ❯ Does your team ensure inclusive imagery, phrasing, and examples are used in D&I learning and development material, and cultural presumptions, references, and stereotypical language are avoided?
- ❯ Does your team ensure that coaching and mentoring processes are transparent and fair. Coaches and mentors should have an understanding of D&I and be matched with participants based on established D&I criteria?

Measures

Examples of relevant D&I measures include:

- ❯ Can you measure the percentage of organizational participation and quantifiable outcomes, including number of sessions attended and duration, and results of knowledge assessments?
- ❯ Can you measure the qualitative outcomes, including development of knowledge, skills, abilities and increased awareness of D&I principles and strategic objectives?
- ❯ Can you measure the percentage of participation of people from underrepresented groups in learning and development activities, including coaching and mentoring?
- ❯ Can you measure the trends in participant feedback, and trends in reported personal and job development?

PERFORMANCE MANAGEMENT

Performance management in a D&I context is a fair and constructive, formal and informal, ongoing process that contributes to the effective management of people and teams to ensure D&I principles are adhered to on an organisational as well as individual level. This can include establishing D&I goals and incentives, as well as reviewing desirable behaviours and outcomes, while mitigating bias and discrimination in performance expectations and assessments.

Outcomes

There is evidence that performance management processes support the D&I principles and strategic objectives. There is evidence that performance management is executed in a fair, impartial and inclusive manner. Discrimination and biases are minimized; job satisfaction is enhanced; and there is evidence that a sense of belonging and engagement is fostered by the organisation, which improves performance. Development needs are identified, and people are provided learning and development opportunities to perform at their best and progress.

Actions

To achieve D&I strategic objectives for performance management, organizations should:

> Does your team ensure that the D&I principles and strategic objectives are included in performance management objectives, and that the focus is on job performance attributes rather than group characteristics?

> Does your team communicate D&I expectations of performance management policies, processes and practices so that they are understandable to all involved in the process, to enable people to achieve D&I goals, and support development of an inclusive workplace?

> Does your team ensure development needs are identified, and learning and development opportunities are provided to people by using a fair, transparent and impartial process?

> Does your team develop an assessment process that ensures people understand their D&I responsibilities and accountabilities, and are provided with relevant feedback and counseling on their performance and behaviour?

> Does your team avoid disparate impact and bias in assessment processes by monitoring performance outcomes by diversity dimensions?

> Does your team review their performance management processes to ensure they are fair, **transparent, and impartial?**

Measures

Examples of relevant D&I measures include:

> Can you analyze people's perception of the fairness of the performance management process?
> Can you identify areas of potential bias or unfairness by analysing performance outcome data and, where they exist, rater assessments, by D&I dimensions?

PAYMENT AND BENEFITS

Pay and benefits policies, processes and practices that ensure fairness and transparency in pay and benefits, equitable and flexible working time and patterns, recognition, leave/time away, and other non-cash provisions, which support the D&I principles and strategic objectives and foster inclusivity.

Outcomes

Pay and benefits policies, processes and practices are equitable and transparent, and support the recruitment, development, and retention of a diverse range of people. People are paid in accordance with equal pay for work of equal value; and diversity dimension related pay gaps are identified and addressed.

Actions

To achieve D&I strategic objectives for pay and benefits, organizations should:

> **Does your** team ensure that policies, processes, and practices include the D&I principles and strategic objectives, and take account of pay negotiations and settlements, including collective employee participation and bargaining (where they exist)?

> Does your team ensure that the process to evaluate and benchmark the relative worth and market value of job roles within the organization is transparent and reflects an equal pay for equal value approach?
> Does your team ensure that information about pay and benefits is communicated in a transparent, understandable, fair, and inclusive manner?
> Does your team ensure that benefits are aligned with the D&I principles and strategic objectives are transparent, understandable, fair, and inclusive, including flexible work and leave arrangements, disability and retirement benefits, and healthcare?
> Does your team make pay and benefits decisions across diversity dimensions in a transparent, fair, inclusive and equitable manner?
> Does your team regularly review the outcomes of pay policies, processes and practices to identify diversity related anomalies and differentials in pay?

Measures

Examples of relevant D&I measures include:

> Can you analyze the data on pay and benefits provided to the workforce by diversity dimension to identify anomalies and differentials in pay and benefits?
> Can you analyze the number, type and diversity dimensions of complaints and disputes related to pay and benefits?
> Can you analyze data from workforce surveys and focus groups to gauge the level of satisfaction and understanding of the organization's pay and benefits, and people's perception of fairness and equity?

SUCCESSION PLANNING

Succession planning based on D&I principles and strategic objectives can enhance workforce development and improve organisational outcomes. An inclusive succession planning process can help people by providing professional development opportunities that enhance organizational capabilities which can strengthen an organization's long-term success. An inclusive succession plan can help ensure that a diverse talent pool is available and enable people to prepare for moving into new job roles as they become available.

Outcomes

Succession planning policies, processes and outcomes are transparent, fair and inclusive. People from underrepresented groups are aware of succession planning opportunities and have access to them. People from underrepresented groups are provided with opportunities to develop the knowledge, skills and abilities required for job roles in the succession plan. The broadest range of people are reflected in succession planning outcomes.

Actions

To achieve D&I strategic objectives for succession planning, organizations should:

> Does your team prioritize the importance of the D&I principles in succession planning policies, processes and practices?
> Does your team identify D&I risks and opportunities, including biases, in the identification of people as potential successors?
> Does your team demonstrate a commitment to a diverse and inclusive workplace by ensuring that people from underrepresented groups are aware of and have access to succession planning opportunities?
> Does your team ensure the broadest range of people with capability and potential are provided with relevant advancement opportunities, and their development is fostered through mentoring and financial support?
> Does your team review succession planning decisions to identify whether underrepresented groups are less likely to be included in succession planning and, if so, identify the barriers and address them?

Measures

Examples of relevant D&I measures include:

> Can you analyze succession planning outcomes to identify D&I dimensions, including areas of potential bias or unfairness?
> Can you review trends in succession planning outcomes to identify impacts on underrepresented groups?
> Can you analyze people's perception of the fairness and outcomes of the succession planning processes?

WORKFORCE MOBILITY

Workforce mobility and the Human Resource Management Life Cycle are interconnected, with workforce mobility applying to periodic assignments, projects and secondments that require relocation, expatriation, inpatriation and repatriation. Processes should utilize an inclusive, proactive, and systematic risk management approach, involving internal and external stakeholders. It can be part of people management processes, including workforce planning, recruitment, performance management, learning and development and succession planning.

Outcomes

Workforce mobility policies, processes and outcomes are transparent, fair and inclusive. People from underrepresented groups are aware of workforce mobility opportunities and have access to them. People from underrepresented groups are provided with opportunities to develop the knowledge, skills and abilities through workforce mobility assignments. The broadest range of people are reflected in workforce mobility outcomes.

Actions

To achieve D&I strategic objectives for workforce mobility, organizations should:

- Does your team prioritize D&I principles in the design and implementation of policies, processes, and practices to ensure an inclusive approach to workforce mobility?
- Does your team ensure that workforce mobility opportunities are fair, equitable and inclusive, and take into account the resources and support required to meet their potentially unique and challenging aspects?
- Does your team communicate and offer opportunities to further develop individual and organisational knowledge through workforce mobility and ensure they are accessible to all, including representation from the broadest range of people?
- Dores your team identify and monitor D&I risks involved with periodic assignments, projects and secondments that require relocation, and expatriation, inpatriation and repatriation?
- Does your team review workforce mobility decisions to identify and ensure the inclusion of underrepresented groups and, if applicable, identify any barriers and address them?

Measures

Examples of relevant D&I measures include:

- Is your team tracking and measuring the trends in workforce mobility and the D&I dimensions of people who are expatriated, inpatriated or repatriated, including turnover, retention, and people's perception of fairness?
- Does your team analyzing the D&I dimensions of proportion of people who accepted and not accepted workforce mobility opportunities, and reasons for none acceptance?

TRANSITION AND REDEPLOYMENT

Transitioning, redeployment, retirement and cessation of employment policies, processes and practices, which support fair, equitable and inclusive outcomes for people in times of economic, organizational and personal change, can foster positive outcomes for the workforce and organization.

Outcomes

Transitioning, redeployment, retirement and cessation of employment policies, processes and outcomes are transparent, fair and inclusive, and mitigate biases and discrimination. The broadest range of people are aware of, and have access to, alternative work and flexible working arrangements. People, including those from underrepresented groups, are aware of transitioning, redeployment, retirement and cessation of employment policies, processes and practices, and are not adversely affected by them. These policies, processes and practices are equitable and transparent. They allow for solicited and unsolicited feedback, and support the transitioning of the broadest range of people into, through and out of the organization.

Actions

To achieve D&I strategic objectives for transitioning, redeployment, retirement and cessation of employment, organizations should:

> Does your team prioritize the D&I principles and strategic objectives in policies, processes, and practices related to transitioning into, through and out of the organization?

> Does your team ensure D&I dimensions of redundancies, redeployment, dismissals, resignations, and retirement are considered?

> Does your team foster an inclusive approach to workforce transitioning offering opportunities for alternative work and flexible working arrangements as people transition into, through and out of the organization?

> Does your team seek feedback from people on their experience with its transitioning processes and practices?

> Does your team monitor and evaluate the impact of workforce transitions on workforce diversity, and ensure that no individuals or groups are more adversely impacted than others?

> Does your team conduct exit interviews to identify trends and signals of potential bias and discrimination; and to ensure that actions for remedial or continuous improvement actions are addressed?

> Does your team investigate claims of potential bias and discrimination in workforce transitioning decision-making processes?

Measures

Examples of relevant D&I measures include:

> Can you calculate the proportion of the workforce transitioning in, through and out of the organization against the whole workforce profile by D&I dimension?
> Can you analyze trends in solicited and unsolicited feedback on transitioning processes and any D&I dimensions identified?
> Can you analyze qualitative data gained from exit interviews to ascertain positive outcomes and adverse impacts resulting from transitioning processes and associated D&I dimensions?
> Can you qualify the number of requests for alternative or flexible working arrangements, or other adjustments, and whether these are granted or denied?
> Can you qualify transitioning options offered by the organization or requested by people, and whether they were accepted or denied, and any associated D&I dimensions?

2.10 PRODUCT AND SERVICES DEVELOPMENT AND DELIVERY

An organization's D&I principles should also be reflected in the development of products and delivery of services in order to identify and recognize the variety of user needs and D&I risks and opportunities. By leveraging a diverse workforce, organizations can develop more inclusive and relevant products and services. A diverse and inclusive workforce can foster creativity that leads to developing innovation. When an organization has a diverse workforce that is representative of the organization's customer base, the development, delivery, and inclusiveness of its products and services may be enhanced.

OUTCOMES

Innovative products and services can be enhanced by engaging a diverse and inclusive workforce during their development and delivery. By leveraging a diverse workforce, organizations can develop more relevant and inclusive products and services. The organization's products and services meet the needs of the broadest range of people, including underrepresented groups. The workforce is given opportunities to provide consultations on the organization's products and services.

ACTIONS

To achieve D&I strategic objectives for Development and Delivery of Products and services, organizations should:

- Does your team prioritize the D&I principles in product and service development?
- Does your team ensure that their workforce diversity is leveraged to facilitate the identification and recognition of the variety of user needs?
- Does your team plan and develop a workforce that represents and recognizes the organization's D&I dimensions of its customer base?
- Does your team consult with D&I related focus groups, committees, workforce representatives, work councils, and labour unions, where they exist, to contribute and share perspectives on products, services, operations, risks and opportunities. Communicate the outcomes of these consultations, as appropriate?
- Does your team incorporate D&I dimensions into customer service policies, processes and practices to ensure that their representatives treat people inclusively?

MEASURES

Examples of relevant D&I measures include:

> Is your team using qualitative and quantitative data to evaluate the needs, outcomes and impacts of products and services on diverse markets and the broadest range of people, including underrepresented groups?

> Can you analyze societal and current customer demographic data to ensure that the broadest range of people have access to the organization's products and services?

> Is your team tracking, monitoring, and documenting the consultations between the organization and its D&I related focus groups, committees, workforce representatives, work councils, and labour unions, where they exist, to gather perspectives about the inclusiveness of its products and services. Utilize the feedback from these consultations to enhance product development and service delivery based on the user's diverse needs?

> Is your team tracking and monitoring the demographic composition of the organization's product development and service delivery teams compared to the customer base?

> Is your team monitoring and analysing solicited and unsolicited feedback for trends, either positive or negative, to ensure that products and services accommodate diverse user needs?

2.11 SUPPLY CHAIN AND OTHER STAKEHOLDERS

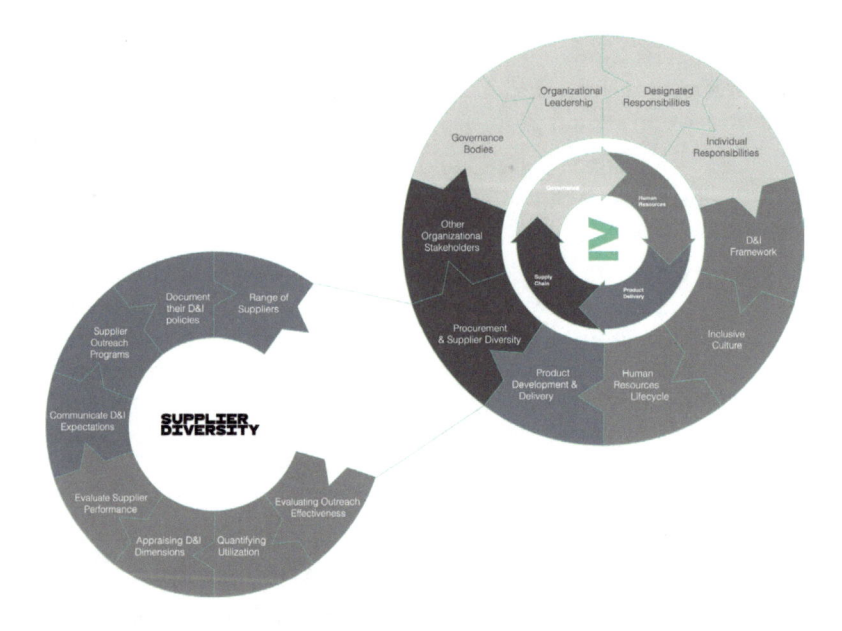

SUPPLIER DIVERSITY

D&I and the organization's procurement and supplier diversity: When organizations rely on third party suppliers to provide a variety of goods and services, and to meet staffing requirements (including contingent workforce), the D&I principles and strategic objectives should be prioritized in procurement processes. This includes tendering, contracting and evaluation stages. In the people management context, applying the organization's D&I principles can enhance the variety of the organization's supplier base and foster inclusiveness in the HR management policies, processes and practices of supply chain partners.

Outcomes

The diversity in the supply chain is evident. Supply chain partners demonstrate commitment to the D&I principles during procurement process stages. The organization's reputation for promoting D&I in the supply chain is recognized. D&I principles are implemented in HR management policies, processes and practices of suppliers..

Actions

To achieve D&I strategic objectives for the organization's procurement and supplier diversity, organizations should:

> - Does your team provide procurement opportunities to the broadest range of suppliers and consider the organization's D&I principles in procurement processes?
> - Does your team identify a variety of potential suppliers, and document their D&I policies, processes, and practices and services?
> - Does your team engage in supplier outreach programs, thereby expanding stakeholder relationships and strengthening community and economic opportunities?
> - Does your team communicate the organization's D&I expectations, including the D&I principles, to potential supply chain partners?

Measures

Examples of relevant D&I measures include:

> - Is your team evaluating supplier performance in meeting the organization's D&I principles at each stage of the procurement process?
> - Is your team appraising and periodically updating the D&I dimensions across the organization's supplier base (at least annually)?
> - Is your team quantifying the organization's utilization and total spend with diverse suppliers?
> - Is your team evaluating the effectiveness of outreach programs and communication activities?

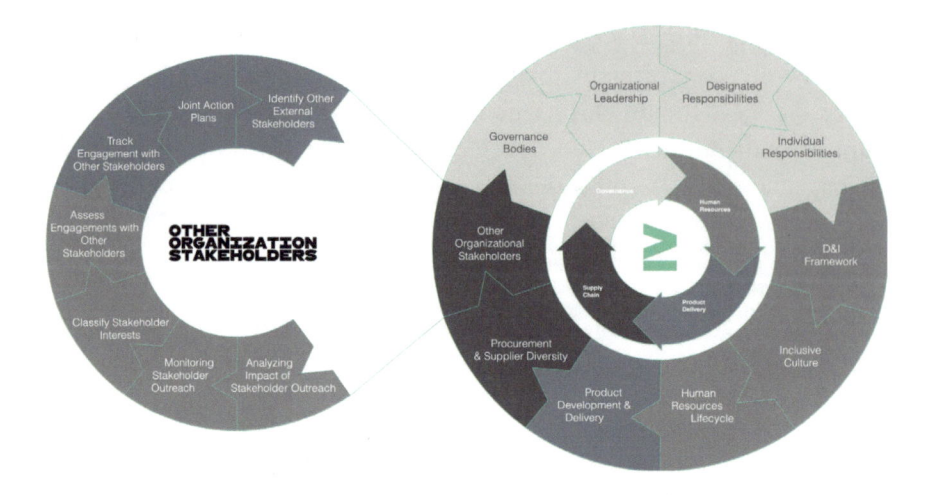

OTHER ORGANIZATIONAL STAKEHOLDERS

D&I AND OTHER ORGANIZATIONAL STAKEHOLDERS

The organization should identify other stakeholders with interests that are related to the D&I framework, as well as social responsibility initiatives and activities, and engage with them in alignment with the D&I principles and strategic objectives.

Other organizational stakeholders include governmental and non-governmental organizations, educational institutions including ancillary bodies such as community outreach and volunteer organizations, alumni associations and academics networks, philanthropic, and occupational federations or professional bodies, and agencies advocating particular interests and for specific causes related to the organization's vision, mission and strategy. These various interests can have a range of consequences for the organization's governance bodies, leadership, those with D&I responsibilities, and the workforce; its suppliers, products and services; and its reputation.

Outcomes

Engagement with for-profit and not-for-profit stakeholders who can contribute to the implementation of the organization's vision, mission and strategy. The organization and stakeholders can jointly develop and implement mutually beneficial D&I action plans.

Actions

To achieve D&I strategic objectives for other organizational stakeholders, organizations should:

> - Does your team identify stakeholders with interests that are related to the vision, mission and strategy of the organization and engage with them in the context with the D&I Framework?
> - Does your team design a process for engagement with stakeholders and record jointly developed action plans (such as external labour union representatives who have authority to negotiate mutually beneficial D&I agreements). Where stakeholders have interests detrimental to the organization's D&I principles and strategic objectives, the organization should maintain a record of risks and opportunities?
> - Does your team design, implement, and track the strategy for engagement with other stakeholders as well as risk mitigation plans associated with stakeholders whose interests are detrimental to the organization's D&I objectives?

Measures

Examples of relevant D&I measures include:

> Is your team assessing the number of engagements and agreements with other stakeholders?

> Is your team classifying the stakeholder's interests based on a scale of impacts on the organization's vision, mission and strategy ranging from positive to negative. This classification can include categories such as stakeholders who enhance the D&I impacts and outcomes of the organization; stakeholders with a neutral influence on D&I impacts and outcomes of the organization; and stakeholders with interests detrimental to the organization's D&I impacts and outcomes?

> Is your team tracking and monitoring outreach activities with other stakeholders from underrepresented groups?

> Is your team analysing the impacts of stakeholders with interests detrimental to the organization's D&I strategic objectives to determine risk factors and apply them accordingly?

PART 2

DIVERSITY & INCLUSION SERVICE DELIVERY

CHAPTER 3
SERVICE PORTFOLIOS & SERVICE CATALOGUES

3.1 SERVICE PORTFOLIO MANAGEMENT

INTRODUCTION

A Service Portfolio describes the services of a provider in terms of business value. It formulates the business need and the service provider's reaction to it. Business values correspond to marketing terms; they assure that the competitiveness of the service provider is measurable with regard to the competitors.

With SPM, managers are better able to assess the quality requirements and accompanying costs. They can look for cost cutting action points, while at the same time maintaining the service quality.

> **Service Portfolio Management (SPM)** *is a dynamic method to govern investments in Service Management across the enterprise, in terms of financial values.*

The goals of Service Portfolio Management are to realize and create maximum value, while at the same time keeping a lid on risks and costs.

SPM starts with documenting the standardized services of the organization and then those of the Service Catalogue. In order to be financially feasible, the portfolio must be a good mix of a Service Catalogue and services in pipeline.

The product manager plays an important role in the Service Portfolio Management. They are responsible for managing services as a product during the entire lifecycle. Product managers coordinate and focus the organization and own the Service Catalogue. They work closely together with the Business Relationship Managers (BRM) and the Business Unit (BU), who coordinate and focus on the Client Portfolio. In essence, SPM is a Governance method.

VALUE FOR THE BUSINESS

The Service Portfolio functions as basis of the Decision-Making Framework. It helps an organization answer the following strategic questions about a client:

*Note a client can be an internal stakeholder or colleague.

- ❯ Why should a client buy these services?
- ❯ Why should a client buy these services from us?
- ❯ What are the price and charge back models?
- ❯ What are our strong and weak points, our priorities and our risks?

> How should our resources and capabilities be allocated?
> A Service Portfolio strategy gives the organization the capability to anticipate changes, while maintaining its strategy and planning.

Activities, methods and techniques

A Service Portfolio describes the services of a provider in terms of business value. He formulates the business need and subsequent reaction by service provider. Business values correspond to marketing terms; they assure that the competitiveness of the service provider can be measured against the competition.

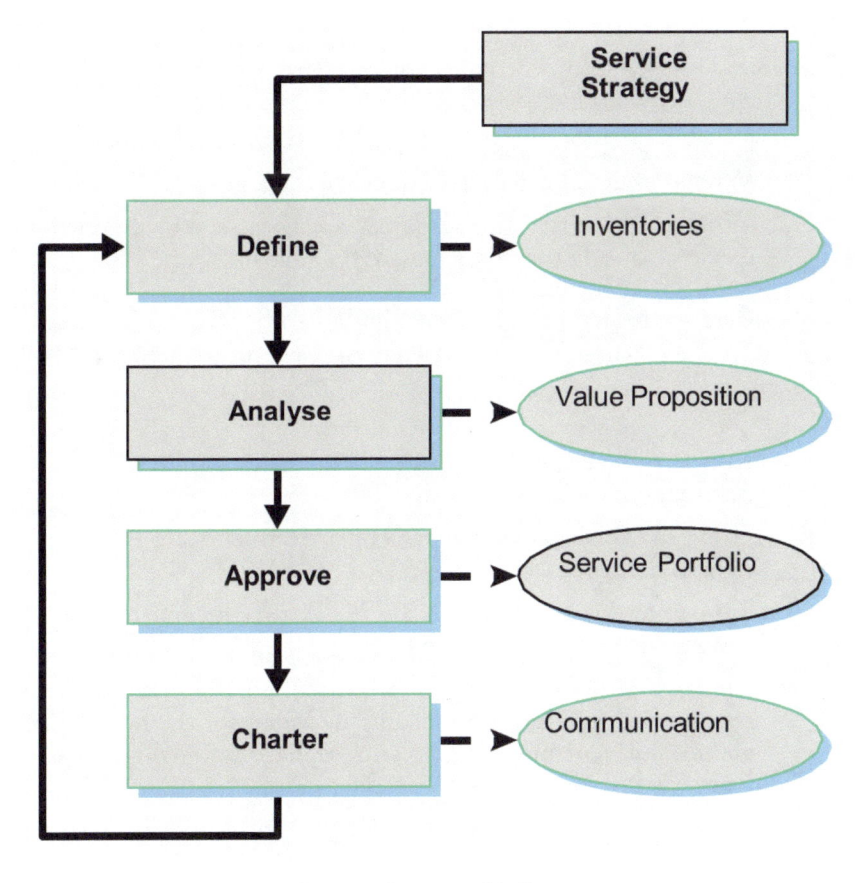

Figure 3.1 Service Portfolio Process

SPM is a dynamic and continuous process that entails the following work methods (see also Figure 3.1):

> Defining - making an inventory of services, business cases and validating the portfolio data; start with collecting information on all existing and proposed services in order to determine the costs of the existing portfolio; the cyclic nature of the SPM process signifies that this phase does not only make the inventory of the services, but also validates the data over and over again; each service in the portfolio should have a business case.

> Analyzing - maximizing the portfolio value, tuning, prioritizing and balancing supply and demand; in this phase, the strategic goals are given a concrete form.

Start with a series of top/down questions such as:

> What are the long-term goals of the service organization?
> Which services are required to realize these goals?
> Which capabilities and resources are necessary to attain these services? In other words, what are the four Ps?

The answers to these questions form the basis of the analysis, but also determine the desired result of SPM. Service investments must be subdivided into three strategic categories:

> Run the Business (RTB) - RTB investments concentrate on maintaining the service production.

> Grow the Business (GTB) - GTB investments are intended to expand the scope of services.

> Transform the Business (TTB) - TTB investments are meant to conquer new markets for products.

> Approving - finishing the proposed portfolio, authorizing services and resources and making decisions for the future; there are six different outcomes: retain, replace, rationalize, refactor, renew and retire.

> Charter - communicating decisions, allocating resources and chartering services; start with a list of decisions and action items; communicate about this clearly and unequivocally with the organization; these decisions must be in tune with the budget

decisions and financial plans; the expected value of each service must have been incorporated into the financial forecasts and resource planning; new services proceed to the Services Design Phase; existing services are renewed in the Service Catalogue.

With an efficient portfolio having optimal ROI and risk levels, an organization creates maximum value while using limited resources and capabilities.

3.2 SERVICE CATALOGUE MANAGEMENT

Remember that a "service" in the context of DISM is one or many of the 4 Project Categories referenced in chapter 2.2.

> ***Service Catalogue Management (SCM)*** *is the development and upkeep of a Service Catalogue that contains all accurate details, the status, possible interactions and mutual dependencies of all present services and those under development.*

VALUE FOR THE BUSINESS

The Service Catalogue is the central resource of all service information. Through the catalogue, everybody in the organization has the services in view which are supplied to the client, how they are delivered, how these services have to be used, for what purpose, and which quality level may be expected by the client.

BASIC CONCEPTS

Over the course of the years, the D&I infrastructures of organizations grow at a steady clip. For this reason, it is difficult to obtain an accurate picture of the services offered by the organizations and whom they are offered to. To get a clearer picture, a Service Portfolio is developed (with a Service Catalogue as part of it), and kept up-to-date. The development of the Service Portfolio is a component of the Service Strategy phase. The Portfolio needs subsequent support from the other phases in the lifecycle.

It is important to make a clear distinction between the Portfolio and the Catalogue:

> **Service Portfolio** - The Portfolio contains information about each service and its status. As a result, the Portfolio describes the entire process, starting with the client requirements for the development, building and execution of the service. The Service Portfolio represents all active and inactive services in the various phases of the lifecycle. For instance using the DISM Lifecycle based on ISO-30415 is a part of the Service Portfolio, but not a part of the Service Catalogue.

> **Service Catalogue** - The Catalogue is a subset of the Service Portfolio and consists only of active and approved services (at retail level) in Service Operation. The Catalogue divides services into components. It contains policies, guidelines and responsibilities, as well as prices, service level arrangements and delivery conditions. The client gets to review the largest part of the Service Catalogue.

By defining every service, a configuration item (CI) must be defined and, when possible, incorporated into a hierarchy, the organization can relate the incidents and Requests for Change to the services in question. It is for this reason that changes in both Portfolio and Catalogue must be part of the change management process.

The Service Catalogue can also be used for a Business Impact Analysis (BIA) as part of D&I Service Continuity Management (DISCM), or as a starting point for the re-distribution of the workload as part of the capacity management. These benefits justify the investment (in time and money) involved in preparing a Catalogue and making it worthwhile.

The Service Catalogue has two aspects:

> **The Business Service Catalogue** - contains all details of the services that are being supplied to the client and the relations with different departments and processes, which are depending on the service. The Business Service Catalogue facilitates the

development of proactive and preventive SLM processes or even the development aimed at Business Service Management (BSM).

- **The Technical Service Catalogue** - contains not only the details of the services supplied to the client, but also their relation to the supporting and shared services, components and CIs. This is the part that is not visible to the client. The Technical Service Catalogue explains which technical aspects (and departments) are necessary to render the service.

A combination of both catalogues provides a quick overview on the impact of the incidents and changes. For this reason, many mature organizations combine both aspects in a Service Catalogue, as part of a Service Portfolio.

Activities, methods and techniques

The Service Catalogue is the only resource which contains constant information about all services of the service provider. The catalogue should be accessible to every authorized person. Activities in this process include:

- defining the services
- producing and maintaining an accurate Service Catalogue
- interaction, mutual dependency and consistency and monitoring the Service Portfolio
- interaction and mutual dependency between the services and supporting services in the Service Catalogue and monitoring the CMS
- interaction and mutual dependency between all services and supporting components and configuration items (CIs) in the Service Catalogue and monitoring the CMS

INTERFACES

Inputs are:

- business information as organization plans
- D&I plans and financial plans
- business impact analysis
- Service Portfolio

Outputs are:

> service definition
> updates for Service Portfolio
> Service Catalogue

METRICS

KPIs are:

> the number of services incorporated into the Service Catalogue and the percentage delivered
> the number of differences discovered between the information from the Service Catalogue and reality
> improvement percentage of the complete Business Service Catalogue, compared with the operational services
> improvement percentage of the complete Technical Service Catalogue, compared with the D&I components in support of the services
> access of the D&I Service Desk to information in support of the services, expressed by the percentage of incidents without this information

IMPLEMENTATION

The most important challenge in the Service Catalogue Management process is maintaining an accurate Service Catalogue (containing both the Business and the Technical aspect) as part of the Service Portfolio. In order to achieve this, spreadsheets or databases must be developed before integrating the Service Catalogue or Service Portfolio into the Configuration Management System (CMS) and Service Knowledge Management System (SKMS). In addition, it is important that all parties involved recognize that both catalogues are essential sources of information which must be used and maintained by everyone in the D&I organization.

Critical Success Factors are:

> accurate Service Catalogue
> users are familiar with the services delivered
> D&I Organization is familiar with the techniques which support the service

Risks include:

> inaccurate information in the Catalogue
> acceptance of the Service Catalogue and its use in the operational processes
> accuracy of the information supplied by the business, D&I and Service Portfolio
> needed help tools to keep the information up-to-date
> access to accurate change management information and processes

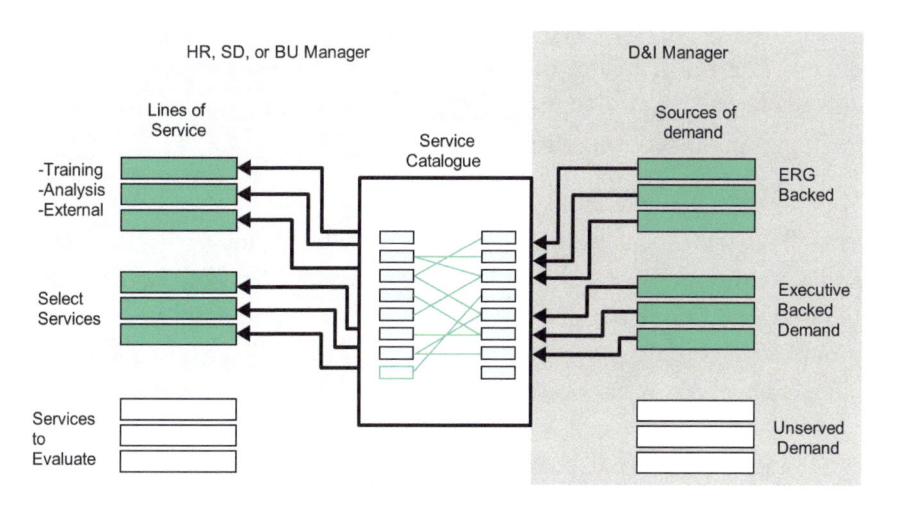

Key: Human Resources (HU), Supplier Diversity (SD), Business Unit (BU)

3.3 SERVICE CATALOGUE USE CASE

If your organization is not using a technology, building a service catalogue is as rudimentary as establish a table (or a spreadsheet) of information with a series of rows and columns that identify the services that your D&I team is aware of.

Let's assume that your organization has a priority to deploy three (3) of the four (4) D&I projects as services across the organization. 1) a survey of some sort 2) a training of some sort and 3) joining a chamber of commerce of some sort. To add more detail to these 3, let's go a step further and assume that your organization will deploy a project to:

> Survey the sentiment of belonging across the organization.
> Train the employees in sexual harassment, to comply with the regulatory mandates that we been in cities like London, Denver, or Mumbai.
> Joining the Disability or LGBT Chamber of Commerce to source more diverse suppliers.

Your service catalogue should demonstrate who owns these project services, as well as, which business unit (BU) they either belong to or influence and any other internal stakeholders, including advisory boards, that affect the budget and roll-out of these programs. For clarity, employee resource groups (ERGs) are a type of advisory board and if your organization already has them, it has also completed the fourth project type.

After identifying what projects you can deploy as services, your team should ask which stakeholders it can pull data from. Stakeholders for instance are departments like Procurement, Product, or Human Resources.

Procurement scenario:

> The Procurement Director wants to know how the suppliers track their engagement of disenfranchised populations, per your region/location.
> DON'T ASK THEM TO ASK CRASS DEMOGRAPHIC QUESTIONS.
> Send them you're a list from your service catalog to see if they have a similar capability to as your organization to identify workplace populations.
> Don't ask how Black or Queer an individual is, unless the institution is giving them an incentive to identify. A safer space, like an ERG is an example of an incentive.

Human Resources scenario:

> A culture crisis has occurred that impacts the company's customers or brand. The Chief Executive tells the Chief HR Officer to help engage the communities or cultures tied t the crisis.
> DON'T COMMIT TO CAPABILITIES YOU DON'T HAVE.
> Joining an Disability Chamber of Commerce before identifying the disables stakeholders (employees and suppliers) in your organization problematic.
> The institution must identify its internal stakeholders to help it engage externally, and add that engagement to the service catalogue.

Product scenario:

> Your product or services is suffering critique from an internal or external stakeholder. It may be a consumer.
> AVOID STATEMENTS WITHOUT INTENTIONALITY
> Organizational accountability is an example of leveraging the existing internal infrastructure, like advisory boards including ERGs, to gain their anonymized feedback on the current state of critique.
> The make a plan to update the product or service version with internal support, at least, and external support, at most.

CAPABILITY:

In this chapter when we mention capabilities, we are specifically referring to the maturity of an organization's ability to deliver the project types across the 32 Domains of D&I per ISO-30415.

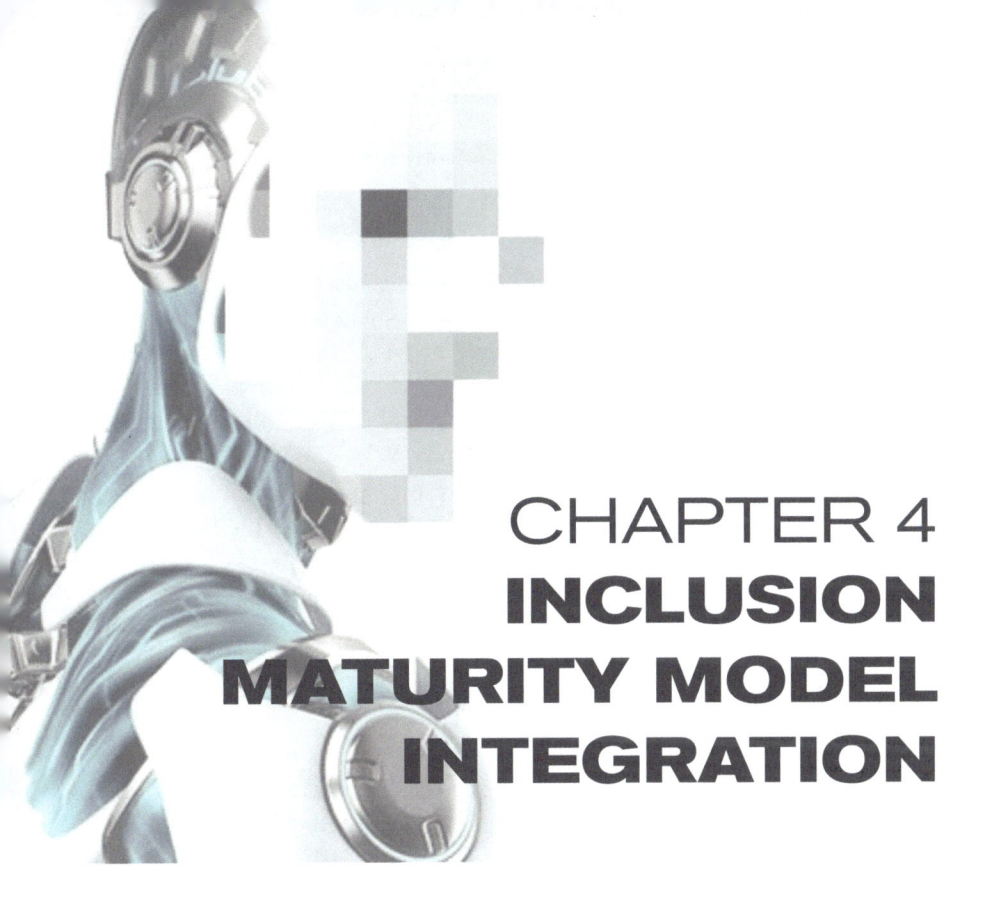

CHAPTER 4
INCLUSION MATURITY MODEL INTEGRATION

4.1 INTRODUCTION

From the moment Richard Nolan introduced his 'staged model' for the application of D&I in organizations in 1973, many people have used stepwise improvement models. These models were quickly recognized as suitable instruments for quality improvement programs, thereby helping organizations to climb up the maturity ladder.

Dozens of variations on the theme can easily be found, ranging from trades such as software development, acquisition, systems engineering, software testing, website development, data warehousing and security engineering, to help desks and knowledge management. Obviously the *kaizen* principle (improvement works best in smaller steps) was one that appealed to many.

> **Kaizen** *is an approach to creating continuous improvement based on the idea that small, ongoing positive changes can reap significant improvements. Typically, it is based on cooperation and commitment and stands in contrast to approaches that use radical or top-down changes to achieve transformation.*

After Nolan's staged model in 1973, the most appealing application of this modeling was found when the Software Engineering Institute (SEI) of Carnegie Mellon University, USA, published its Software Capability Maturity Model (SW-CMM). The CMM was copied and applied in most of the cases mentioned above, making CMM something of a standard in maturity modeling. The CMM was later followed by newer editions, including CMMI (CMM Integrated).

Later, these models were applied in quality management models, like the European Foundation for Quality Management (EFQM). Apart from the broad quality management models, there are several other industry accepted practices, such as Six Sigma and TQM, which are complementary to ISO-30415.

The available standards, and frameworks of best practice, offer guidance for organizations in achieving 'operational excellence' in D&I Service Management. Depending upon their stage of development, organizations tend to require different kinds of guidance.

Maturity model: CMMI

In the D&I industry, the process maturity improvement process is best known in the context of the **Capability Maturity Model Integration (CMMI)**. This process improvement method was developed by the Software Engineering Institute (SEI) of Carnegie Mellon University. CMMI provides both a staged and a continuous model. In the continuous representation, improvement is measured using capability levels.

> *Maturity* is measured for a particular process across an organization.

In the staged representation, improvement is measured using maturity levels, for a set of processes across an organization.

The usual capability levels in the **CMMI continuous representation** are:

1. **Incomplete process** - a process that either is not performed or partially performed
2. **Performed process** - satisfies the specific goals of the process area
3. **Managed process** - a performed (capability level 1) process that has the basic infrastructure in place to support the process.
4. **Defined process** - a managed (capability level 2) process that is tailored from the organization's set of standard processes according to the organization's tailoring guidelines, and contributes work products, measures and other process improvement information to the organizational process assets
5. **Quantitatively Managed process** - a defined (capability level 3) process that is controlled using statistical and other quantitative techniques
6. **Optimizing process** - a quantitatively managed (capability level 4) process that is improved based on an understanding of the common causes of variation inherent in the process

The **CMMI staged representation** model defines five maturity levels, each a layer in the base for the next phase in the ongoing process improvement, designated by the numbers 1 through 5:

1. **Initial** - processes are ad hoc and chaotic

2. **Managed** - the projects of the organization have ensured that processes are planned and executed in accordance with policy
3. **Defined** - processes are well characterized and understood, and are described in standards, procedures, tools and methods
4. **Quantitatively Managed** - the organization and projects establish quantitative objectives for quality and process performance, and use them as criteria in managing processes
5. **Optimizing** - focuses on continually improving process performance through incremental and innovative process and technological improvements

Many other maturity models were based on these structures, such as the **Gartner** Maturity Models. Most of these models are focused at capability maturity. Some others, like **KPMG's** World Class IT Maturity Model, take a different approach.

STANDARD: ISO-30415

Developing and maintaining a quality system which complies with the requirements of the ISO 9000 (ISO-9000:2000) series can be considered a tool for the organization to reach and maintain the system-focused (or 'managed' in D&I Service CMM) level of maturity. These ISO standards emphasize the definition, description and design of processes. For D&I Service Management organizations, a specific ISO standard was produced: the ISO-30415. It reflects other service models that deploy agreed upon standards in other professions. After a profession is agreed upon, it must be deployed as an auxiliary operational offering (see Figure 4.1).

CUSTOMER MATURITY

When assessing the maturity of an organization, we cannot restrict ourselves to the service provider. The **level of maturity of the customer** (Figure 4.2) is also important. If there are large differences in maturity between the provider and the customer, then these will have to be considered to prevent a mismatch in the approach, methods and mutual expectations. Specifically, this affects the communication between the customer and the provider.

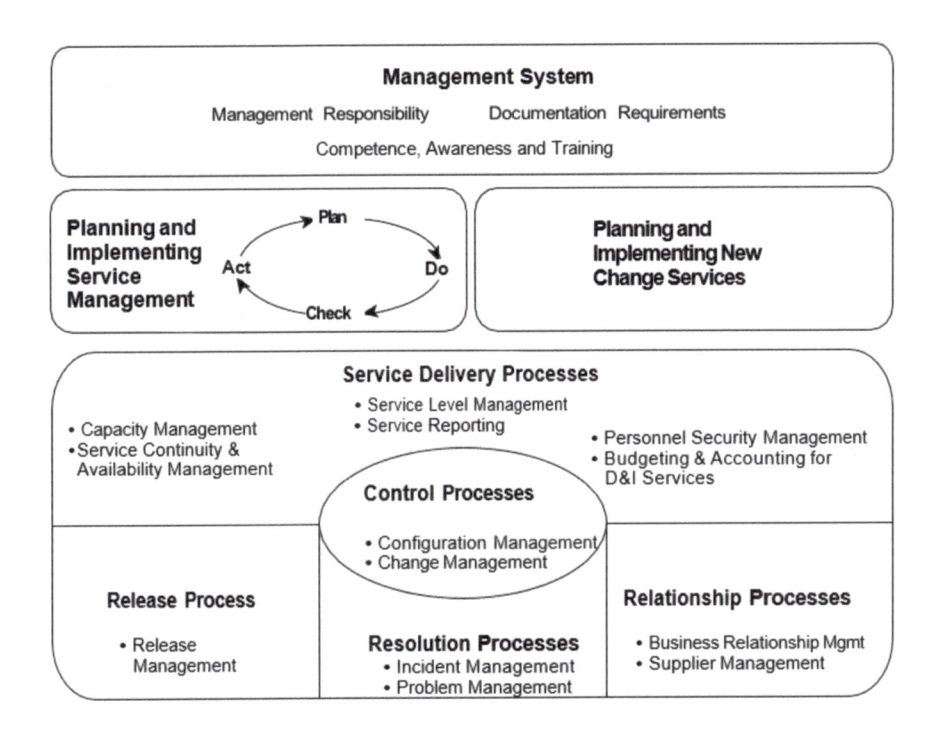

Figure 4.1   Overview of the ISO-30415 Service Management System

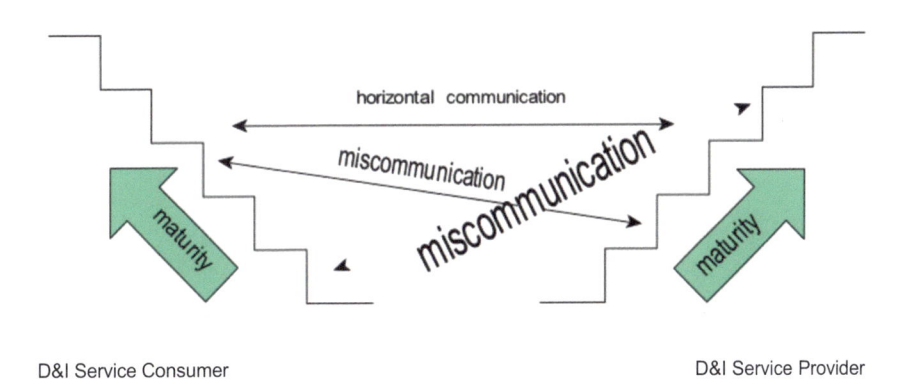

Figure 4.2   Communication and maturity levels: customer and provider

Historically, Maturity Models have started with at least 5 levels of maturity, but because of the fledgling nature of Diversity & Inclusion as a discipline we recommend 4. In 2023 D&I is not what we would call a rigorous discipline, it is a regular reaction to crisis. That can change as we standardize. The D&I CMM or **Inclusion Maturity Model Integration** ® (IMMI) score is supposed to demonstrate ongoing commitment to valuing diversity and inclusion (D&I) that should be fostered by governing bodies and leaders. The ISO/DIS 30415:2021 standard is using the following process improvement chart in figure 2.

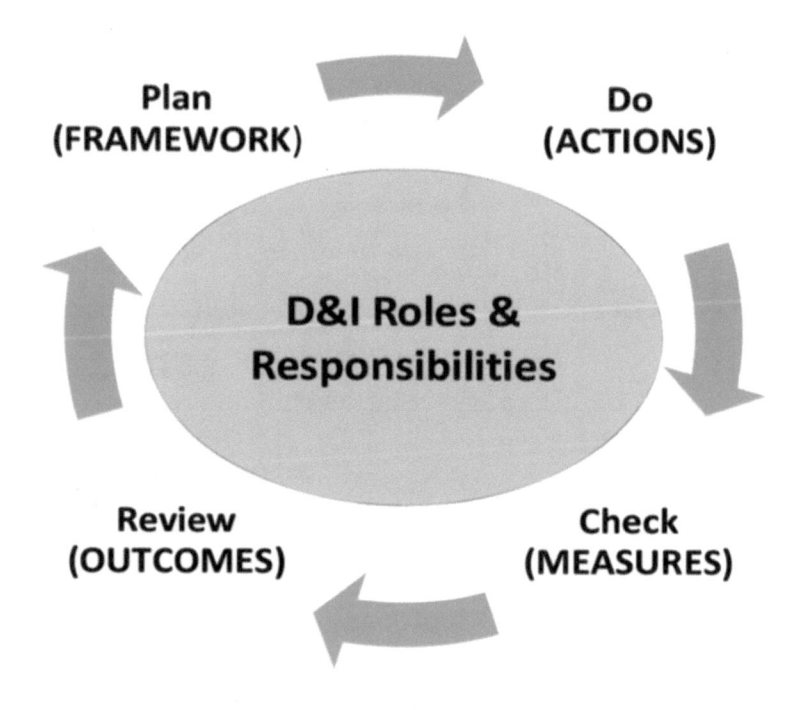

Figure 4.3   Plan Do Check Act Lifecycle

As indicated in the chart above, there are several repeatable steps to improve the D&I posture. Starting with providing guidance on D&I Roles and Responsibilities, a plan/framework can be set up which includes a set of Actions (Do) and Measures (Check) to foster development of an inclusive workplace.

To calculate an IMM score, our approach assigns ISO/DIS 30415 controls for Roles & Responsibilities, Actions and Measures to "CMM-like" domains. Doing so, this enables an organization to determine and optimize its "D&I posture" by measuring the current state of achievement.

In the framework of Diversity & Inclusion Service Management (DISM) we have defined a total of 4 domains for Roles & Responsibilities, and a total of 14 domains each for Actions and Measures. The table below shows the definition of individual D&I domains. In total we recognize 32 risk domains where an organization can have a lack-of-inclusion in, leaving the organization vulnerable.

		D&I Roles and Responsibilities
	1	Governance Bodies
	2	Organizational Leadership
	3	Designated Responsibilities for D&I
	4	Individual Responsibilities
		D&I Actions and Measures
	1	Diversity and Inclusion (D&I) Framework
	2	Inclusive Culture
	3	HR Mgmt Life Cycle / Workforce Planning
	4	HR Mgmt Life Cycle / Recruitment
	5	HR Mgmt Life Cycle / Onboarding and induction
	6	HR Mgmt Life Cycle / Learning and development
	7	HR Mgmt Life Cycle / Performance management
	8	HR Mgmt Life Cycle / Pay and benefits
	9	HR Mgmt Life Cycle / Succession Planning
	10	HR Mgmt Life Cycle / Workforce Mobility
	11	HR Mgmt Life Cycle / Transition, Redeployment, Retirement and Cessation of Employment Policies
	12	D&I and Development and Delivery of Products and services
	13	D&I and Organizational Procurement
	14	D&I and other organizational stakeholders

Figure 4.4   Grouping of D&I Controls

In our system, each control domain is described by a capability/maturity level scale from 1 to 4, as described in the definition below. In the literature (see figure 1), often a five level IMMI score is used; in our approach, however, we combine level 4 (quantitatively managed) and level 5 (optimizing) in a single level 4 as described below.

To determine the IMMI score for a domain, a company's representative must complete an assessment questionnaire; maturity levels from 1 – 3 are self-assessed but to achieve the highest level of maturity (level 4) in our model, evidence (e.g. policy, KPIs or measurements) must be submitted to the platform then reviewed by an independent, third party analyst. An additional point will be awarded if the submission meets all requirements.

Level 1: Ad hoc (initial)

Some D&I initiatives are taken, but there is minimal measurement, methodology and strategy, action is reactive.

Level 2: Learning (managed)

The Company begins to structure and organize around a coherent D&I strategy, but sometimes still reactive.

Level 3: Under control (defined)

The Company manages processes and proactively implements robust controls.

Level 4: Measured (quantitatively managed and optimizing)

The Company maintains a strategic advantage over competitors with controlled, measured and continuously reviewed D&I processes.

4.2 2021-23 INCLUSION MATURITY MODEL INTEGRATION

Because of the fledgling nature of D&I standardization and the ISO standard, our earliest case studies proved that the normal steps in a CMMI were too daunting for diversity and inclusion practitioners between the years of 2021 and 2023. Our committed of advisors at DISM Forum decided that based on user experiences across ~300 organizations that 4 levels of maturity including a 0th level was necessary to get D&I

practitioners used to delivering D&I in the same that organizations deliver other products and services internally.

We even asked ChatGPT. The GPT which stands for Generative Pre-trained Transformer. It's a family of artificial intelligence language models, which was introduced in 2018 by the American artificial intelligence organization OpenAI. It is a type of deep learning model used to generate human-like text.

Can you outline a Capability Maturity Model Integration for Diversity & Inclusion?

Yes, I can provide an outline for a Capability Maturity Model Integration (CMMI) for Diversity & Inclusion (D&I).

The CMMI is a process improvement model that helps organizations improve their processes and achieve their goals. It is based on best practices and can be used to assess and improve an organization's capability to deliver high-quality products and services.

The CMMI for D&I can help organizations assess and improve their D&I practices and policies. Here is an outline for the model:

Level 1: Initial

At this level, the organization has no formal D&I practices or policies in place. There may be some ad-hoc efforts to promote diversity and inclusion, but they are not consistent or comprehensive.

Level 2: Managed

At this level, the organization has established some formal D&I practices and policies. There is a D&I committee or task force responsible for overseeing D&I efforts, and there are some basic D&I training programs in place. The organization may have a diversity statement and a code of conduct that includes D&I principles.

Level 3: Defined

At this level, the organization has a well-defined D&I program that is integrated into its overall business strategy. There are clear goals and metrics for measuring D&I progress, and the organization has established a D&I culture that is embraced by all employees. D&I training programs are mandatory for all employees, and the organization has implemented D&I best practices throughout its operations.

Level 4: Quantitatively Managed

At this level, the organization has a data-driven approach to D&I. It collects and analyzes data on D&I performance, and uses that data to continuously improve its D&I program. The organization has established a D&I dashboard that provides real-time data on D&I metrics, and it has implemented a system for tracking and addressing D&I complaints and concerns.

Level 5: Optimizing

At this level, the organization has achieved a high level of D&I maturity. It is constantly seeking ways to innovate and improve its D&I program, and it has established a culture of inclusion that extends beyond the workplace. The organization is recognized as a leader in D&I, and it actively shares its best practices and knowledge with others.

Overall, the CMMI for D&I provides a framework for organizations to assess and improve their D&I practices and policies. By adopting this model, organizations can create a more inclusive workplace, improve employee engagement and retention, and enhance their reputation as a socially responsible organization.

This is not the model that we used but it was surprisingly close.

4.3 BENEFITS AND RISKS OF DISM FRAMEWORKS

The list below identifies some benefits and possible problems of using D&I Service Management best practices. This list is not intended to be definitive, but is provided here as a basis for considering some of the benefits that can be achieved and some of the mistakes that can be made when using common process-based D&I Service Management frameworks

Benefits to the customer/user:

> the provision of D&I Services becomes more customer-focused and agreements about service quality improve the relationship
> the services are described better, in customer language, and in more appropriate detail
> better management of the quality, availability, reliability and cost of the services are managed better
> communication with the D&I organization is improved by agreeing on the points of contact

Benefits to the D&I organization:

> the D&I organization develops a clearer structure, becomes more efficient, and is more focused on the corporate objectives
> the D&I organization is more in control of the infrastructure and services it has responsibility for, and changes become easier to manage
> an effective process structure provides a framework for the effective outsourcing of elements of the D&I Services
> following best practices encourages a cultural change towards providing service, and supports the introduction of quality management systems based on the ISO 9000 series or on ISO-30415
> frameworks can provide coherent frames of reference for internal communication and communication with suppliers, and for the standardization and identification of procedures

| 117

Potential problems/mistakes:

- the introduction can take a long time and require significant effort, and may require a change of culture in the organization; an overambitious introduction can lead to frustration because the objectives are never met

- if process structures become an objective in themselves, the service quality may be adversely affected; in this scenario, unnecessary or over-engineered procedures are seen as bureaucratic obstacles, which are to be avoided where possible

- there is no improvement in D&I Services due a fundamental lack of understanding about what the relevant processes should provide, what the appropriate performance indicators are, and how processes can be controlled

- improvement in the provision of services and cost reductions are insufficiently visible, because no baseline data was available for comparison and/or the wrong targets were identified

- a successful implementation requires the involvement and commitment of personnel at all levels in the organization; leaving the development of the process structures to a specialist department may isolate that department in the organization and it may set a direction that is not accepted by other departments

- if there is insufficient investment in appropriate training and support tools, justice will not be done to the processes and the service will not be improved; additional resources and personnel may be needed in the short term if the organization is already overloaded by routine D&I Service Management activities which may not be using 'best practices'

4.4 BENEFITS

Process activities are not limited to one part of the organization. Because of this the process manager must map the defined process roles and activities to existing staff. Clear definitions of the responsibility and accountability are required, for instance in a **RACI matrix** (*Responsible, Accountable, Consulted, Informed*).

Roles and responsibilities:

Continual Service Improvement (CSI) knows permanent production roles such as **service manager, service owner, process owner** and analysts, and temporary project roles such as project managers and project team members. Figure 4.5 provides an overview of the accompanying key activities and roles. Not all roles are full-time. Make a global division and adjust this later on if needed.

Key activity	Key role
Gather data from the measurement of service results and service management processes and compare these to the starting point (baseline), goals, Service Level Agreements (SLAs) and benchmarks; analyze trends	Service manager, service owner, D&I process owner
Set targets for efficiency improvement and cost effectiveness throughout the entire Service Lifecycle	Service manager
Set targets for service improvements and use of resources	Service manager, service owner, business process owner

Figure 4.5 Key activities and the roles to be divided

Key activity	Key role
Consider new business and security requirements	Service manager, business process owner
Create an Systems Improvement Plan (SIP) and implement improvements	Service manager, service owner, process owner
Enable personnel to propose improvements	Service manager

Measure, report and communicate about improvement initiatives	Service manager
Revise policy, processes, procedures and plans if needed	Service manager
Ensure that all approved actions are completed and that they achieve the desired result	Service manager, business manager, D&I process owner, business process owner

Figure 4.6 provides an overview of the roles, activities and skills needed for the different steps in the Continual Service Improvement (CSI) improvement process.

Step	Roles	Activity types	Skills
1. What should you measure?	Decision makers, such as the service manager, service owner, service level manager, CSI manager, process owner	• high management level • high variation • action oriented • communicative • focus on future	• management skills • communicate • create and use concepts • handle complex and uncertain situations • education and • experience
2. What can you measure?	Internal and external service providers who know the possibilities, such as the service manager, service owner, process owner and the process manager	• intellectual • investigative • medium to high variation • goal oriented • specialized in business management	• analyze • model • inventive attitude • education • program

Step	Roles	Activity types	Skills
3. Gather data (measure)	Personnel who supply services in the Service Transition and Service Operation life phases, such as the D&I Service Desk personnel on a daily basis	• standardized • routine (low variation) • automated • clerical level • procedural	• accuracy • precision • applied training • technical experience
4. Process data	See step 3	• specialized • structures • automated • medium variation • procedural	• numerical skills • methodical • accurate • applied training • programming • experience with tools
5. Analyze data	Internal and external service providers who know the possibilities, such as the service owner, process owner and the business and D&I analysts	See step 2	See step 2

Figure 4.7 Roles for the CSI improvement process

Step	Roles	Activity types	Skills
6. Present and use the information (reporting)	Internal and external service providers who know the possibilities and the main decision makers, such as the **CSI manager, service manager, service owner, service level manager, process owner**	See step 1	See step 1
7. Implement corrective actions	See step 6	See step 2	See step 2

121

For the ISO-30415 Foundations exam, knowledge is required on the roles printed in bold in Figure 4.7. We will discuss these further, except for the role of **service level manager**. The Section on 'Service Design' describes this role. The Section 'Other roles' mentions other roles present in CSI. Figure 4.8 shows how the various roles can co-operate.

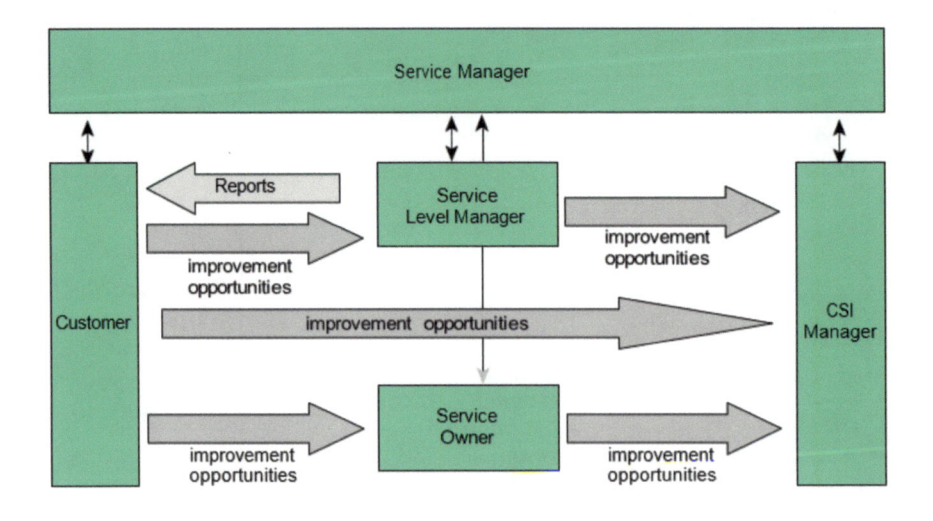

Figure 4.8 How the various roles co-operate effectively

SERVICE MANAGER

The service manager co-ordinates the development, introduction and evaluation of one or more products or services. He is responsible for:

> achieving company strategy and goals
> benchmarking
> financial management
> customer management
> vendor management
> full lifecycle management
> investor management

He must know a great deal about market analysis, be able to anticipate new market needs, formulate complex programs, guide his personnel and sell his services.

CSI MANAGER

Without a clear and unambiguous responsibility improvement will not occur. As a result this new role is essential for a successful improvement program. The CSI manager is responsible for CSI in the organization. He manages the measuring, analysis, investigating and reporting of trends and initiates service improvement activities. In addition, he also makes sure that sufficient CSI supporting resources are available. He is responsible for:

- successful introduction of CSI in the whole lifecycle
- awareness of CSI in the organization
- allocating CSI roles
- identifying and presenting improvement opportunities to higher management and prioritizing them together with the service owner
- defining monitoring demands together with the service level manager
- taking care that the proper monitoring tools are installed
- creating SIPs together with the service level manager
- setting starting points (doing baseline measurements)
- defining CSFs, KPIs and metrics
- using supporting frameworks and models
- making knowledge management a permanent part of the daily routine
- evaluating analyzed data

The CSI manager must be able to lead projects throughout the organization, build good relationships with the business and the D&I management, have a flair for improvement opportunities throughout the company and be able to counsel staff.

SERVICE OWNER

It is crucial to appoint one person responsible for each service: this is the **service owner**. He is the central point of contact for a specific service. It does not matter where the underlying technological components, process or functions are located. His main responsibilities are:

> owning and representing the service
> understanding which components make up the service
> measuring the performance and availability
> attending *Change Advisory Board* (CAB) meetings if these changes are relevant to his service
> passing improvement opportunities for his service to the CSI manager and helping to prioritize these
> taking part in internal and external service evaluations
> maintaining the service description in the Service Catalogue
> negotiating about SLAs and OLAs

PROCESS OWNER

Having an owner is just as crucial to a process as to a service. The **process owner** ensures that the organization follows a process. He must be a senior manager with enough credibility, influence and authority in the organization departments which are part of the process. He must already be appointed in the process design phase and be both the coach and the main advocate of the process. See also the Section on 'Service Design'.

OTHER ROLES

Other roles which are important to CSI:

> **Service knowledge manager** - designs and maintains a knowledge management strategy and implements this
> **Reporting analyst** - evaluates and analyzes data, and spots trends; often co-operates with SLM roles (see Service Design); must have good communication skills because reporting is a type of communication
> **Communication role** - designs a communication strategy for CSI

4.5 METHODS TECHNIQUES, AND TOOLS

There are various methods and techniques to check whether planned improvements actually produce measurable improvements. One method or technique is not usually enough: you need to find the best mix for your organization. Check whether the chosen methods and techniques are suitable to measure the results of your processes, document them thoroughly and instruct staff who will be using the method or technique.

IMPLEMENTATION REVIEW

To determine whether the improvements produce the desired effects, you have to ask whether the original problem situation has actually improved, and how the organization has planned and implemented the improvement. The following questions help with this:

> Have we correctly assessed the present situation and have we properly formulated the problem?
> Have we taken the correct decisions with respect to our strategy?
> Have we adopted the strategy in the right way?
> Have we formulated the right CSI goals?
> Have the goals been reached?
> Do we now provide better D&I Services?
> What are the lessons learned and where are we now?

ASSESSMENTS

An assessment compares the performance of a process against a performance standard. This can be an agreement in an SLA (service level agreement), a maturity standard, or an average of companies in the same industry. In this last case, this refers to a benchmark. With assessments D&I organizations show their commitment to maturity.

Assessments are very well suited to answer the question 'where are we now?', and to determine the extent of the gap with 'where we want to be'. Using an accepted framework will help benchmarking the maturity. Keep in mind that the desired performance or maturity level of a process depends on the impact that the process has on the customer's business processes.

First determine the relationship between business processes, D&I Services, D&I systems and components. CSI can separately assess the effectiveness and efficiency results for each component. This helps in identifying areas for improvement.

It is crucial to delineate clearly what is being assessed. Base this on the goals and the expected use of the reports. An assessment can take place on three levels:

> **process only** - only assess process components from the process description
> **people, process and technology** - also assess skills, roles and talents of managers and staff who participate in the process; also assess the process-supporting technology
> **complete** - also assess the ability and preparedness for process acceptance and the possibility of formulating and following a process strategy and goals

All these can be compared to the selected maturity model. Assessments are useful in the:

> **planning phase** - as starting point (baseline) for process performance
> **implementation phase** (*do*) - to check that the estimates are correct
> **measurement phase** (*check*) - to complete the balance and to identify further possible improvements

ADVANTAGES OF ASSESSMENTS:

> they can measure certain parts of a process independently of the rest and determine the impact of that specific component on the rest of the process

> they can be repeated

DISADVANTAGES OF ASSESSMENTS:

> they only offer a picture of one moment and do not give insight into the cultural dynamic of an organization

> they can become a goal in themselves instead of a means

> they are labour intensive

> the results are still dependent on subjective assessors and therefore not entirely objective, even if the measurements are

This applies to both internal and external assessments. Table 7.3 gives an overview of the advantages and disadvantages of both forms.

BENCHMARKS

A benchmark is a special type of assessment: organizations compare (parts of) their processes with the performance of the same types of processes that are commonly recognized as 'best practice'. This can be done in four ways:

> **internal** - against an earlier starting point (baseline)

> **internal** - against another system or department

Internal assessment	
Advantages	**Disadvantages**
• no expensive consultants • self-assessment sets are available for free • promotes internal co-operation and communication • promotes internal level of knowledge • good starting point for CSI • internal knowledge of existing environment	• less objective • disappointing acceptance of findings • internal politics can get involved • limited knowledge of skills • labor intensive
External assessment	
Advantages	**Disadvantages**
• objectivity • expert ISO-30415 knowledge • wide experience with several D&I organizations • analytical skills • credibility • minimal impact on the provision of services	• high costs • risk as to acceptance • limited knowledge of existing environments • insufficient preparation limits effectiveness

Figure 4.9 Internal versus external assessment

> **external** - against industry standards
> **external** - directly with similar organizations; this is only useful, however, if there are enough similar organizations in terms of environment, sector and geographical placement

The form you choose depends on the purpose of the benchmark:

> measurements of costs (price) and performance of internal or external service providers
> compare process performance with the existing industry standard
> compare the financial performance of global D&I costs with industry standard or other organizations
> measure effectiveness in achieving the required customer satisfaction

To determine this you can set up an organizational profile, which consists of four key components:

> **business profile** - basic information such as scope and type
> **present assets** - hardware such as desktops and servers
> **present best practices** - policy, procedures and tools and the degree to which they are used in the organization
> **complexity** - the number of end users and the quantity and type of technology in your organization

In all cases a benchmark provides the following results:

> represents performance
> shows the gaps
> shows the risk of not closing these gaps
> helps set priorities
> helps in communicating the information well

In this way organizations discover whether their processes are cost effective, whether they fulfill customer needs and how effective they are in comparison to other organizations. They become aware of the need to improve and the ways they can do so, for example in the areas of economies of scale, efficiency and effectiveness. Management can then act on this. In the ideal case benchmarking forms part of a continual cycle of improvement and is repeated regularly.

Studies into the performance of one's own and other departments or organizations take time. Setting up a benchmark database and visiting other organizations also involves costs.

Benchmarking is done in co-operation with:

- the business
- users or costumers
- internal service providers
- external service providers
- users in 'public space'
- benchmark partners (other organizations who are involved in the comparison)

First look to see if there are any problem areas. Use the steps from the CSI improvement process, supported by (some of) the following techniques:

- informal discussions with the business, staff or suppliers
- focus groups
- market research
- quantitative research
- surveys
- re-engineering analysis
- process files
- quality control variation reports
- financial ratio analysis

Two special forms of benchmarking are:

- **Process maturity comparison** - as opposed to an assessment, this is not a comparison with the maturity model, but the maturity level is compared with that of other organizations; for example, CMMI can be used as a maturity model

> **Total cost of ownership (TCO)** - the sum of all the costs of the design, the introduction, operation and improvement of services (introduced by Gartner); it is often used to compare specific services in one organization with those of another organization

BALANCED SCORECARD (BSC)

Kaplan and Norton developed the **Balanced Scorecard (BSC)** in the 1990s. Define a Balanced Scorecard for each business unit. Begin carefully: select two to four goals. Then you can extend this as a 'waterfall' to the underlying components, such as the D&I Service Desk. After successful implementation keep measuring regularly.

GAP ANALYSIS

This analysis naturally arises from assessments and benchmarks. It determines where the organization is now and the size of the gap with where it wants to be. In this way light is shed on new opportunities for improvement. The service gap model in Figure 4.10 shows possible gaps or discrepancies.

Gap analyses can be the result of a benchmarking on service or process maturity investigations. They can be done on a strategic, tactical or operational level. It gives an overview of the amount of resources and money which an organization has to spend to reach specific goals.

SWOT-ANALYSIS

A SWOT-analysis looks at the Strengths, Weaknesses, Opportunities and Threats of an organization (component) or project. The organization then answers the following questions:

> How can we profit from strong points?
> How can we remove weak points?
> How can we use opportunities optimally?
> How can we manage and eliminate threats?

Set your end goal before you perform a SWOT analysis. Look at which strong points help achieve a goal, which weaknesses prevent you from doing this, what external conditions promote the goal, and what external conditions prevent it.

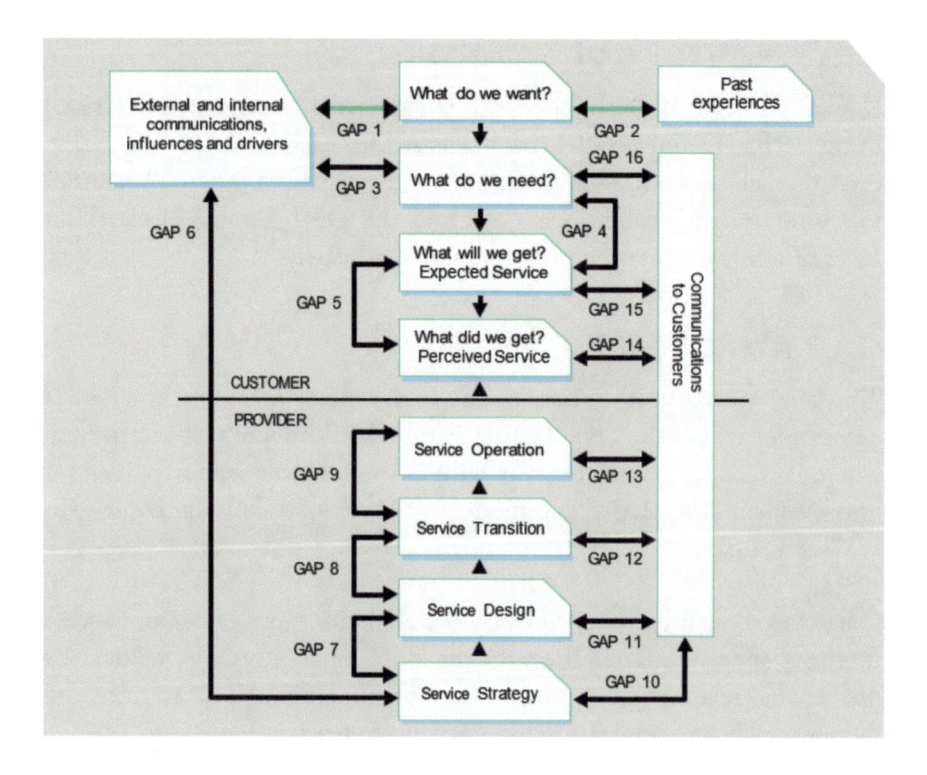

Figure 4.10 Service gap model (after SERVQUAL: Parasuraman, Zeithaml and Berry)

To arrive at a SWOT of the whole organization, you can first make a SWOT for each organization component or function and then integrate them into a company SWOT. See Table 7.4 for sample aspects of SWOTs.

Possible strengths	**Possible weaknesses**
• core competences • financial means • recognized as a market leader • proven management	• no clear strategic direction • outdated facilities • low profits • little insight into performance
Possible opportunities	**Possible threats**
• creation of new customer groups • application of skills and knowledge for new products	• foreign competition with lower prices • lower market growth • expensive legislation and regulation

Figure 4.11   Examples of aspects from SWOT analyses

Rummler-Brache swim-lane diagram

Geary Rummler and Alan Brache introduced the idea of representing the relationships between processes and organizations or departments with 'swim lanes' in a Rummler-Brache swim-lane diagram. This maps the flow of a process: from the customer through the department to the technology (Figure 4.11). The horizontal rows divide the separate organizations or departments from each other. Activities and decisions are connected through arrows to indicate the flow.

The row in which these components are placed indicates which organizational component is responsible for the activity or decision.

Because this instrument places the whole process within a recognizable structure of organizations, it is very useful as a communication tool with the management.

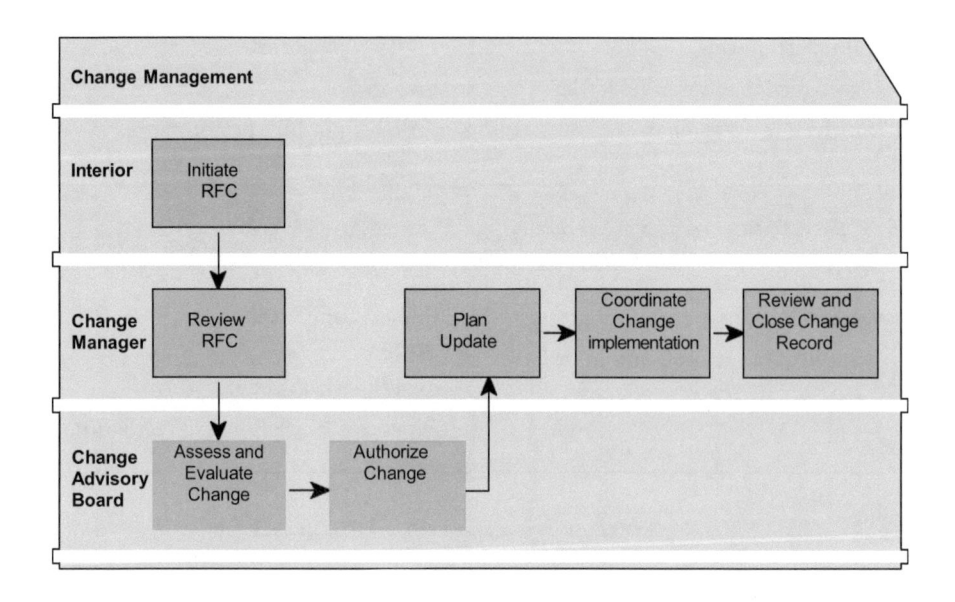

Figure 4.11   Rummler-Brache swim-lane diagram

Tools

CSI needs different types of software to support, test, monitor and report on the DISM processes. The selection of tools forms part of the question 'where do we want to be?' Ultimately the business must provide the answer to this question by means of goals, determining the need for software tools.

In any case, tools must monitor and analyze the most important components of a service, in a manner that supports the CSI Improvement Process. They can also centralize, automate and integrate the key processes. This then produces new data for trend analysis.

Tools to be used for CSI are for example:

› **D&I Service Management packages** - follow all activities using one database; as a result the consequences for service delivery and relations between the activities can be determined; the configuration management system (CMS) integrates all tools and provides critical data on improvement opportunities

› **Event management** - events are status reports from, for example, servers and systems; tools for event management assess these status reports for impact and origin, and categorize the reports

› **System and network management** - monitors technology platforms; the tools generate error messages for event management, providing input to performance management

› **Automated incident and problem solving** - proactive tracing monitors, pre-programmed scripts that automatically repair the technology; they also record information for analysis for possible improvements

› **Knowledge management** - databases with descriptions of earlier incidents and problems, and their proven solutions; also measurement of the use of the database and the effectiveness of the solution

› **Service Request processing (Service Catalogue and workflow)** - helps with defining a Service Catalogue and automates Service Requests and their settlement

› **Performance management** - collects data about availability, capacity and performance to develop availability and capacity information systems

› **Application and service performance monitoring** - monitors the service of the technology as far as the customer; the tools measure availability, reaction and transaction times and efficiency of the servers

› **Statistical analysis instruments** - central collection point for raw data from the above tools; the analysis instruments group these data logically, creating models for present services and making predictive models for future services

› **Software version management/software configuration management** - creates an overview of all

software for the development environment, thus providing the Definitive Media Library (DML)
- **Software test management** - supports the test and roll-out activities of release management
- **Security management** - protects against intruders and unauthorized use; all hardware and software that is under security management must automatically give a warning as soon as a security incident threatens
- **Project and portfolio management** - registers new functionality and the services and systems that they support; the tools help to map the Service Portfolio and keep it up-to-date; they can also automate organizational aspects such as plans
- **Financial management** - monitors the use of resources and services for the invoicing process
- **Business intelligence/reporting** - collects data from all the above mentioned tools, with which it generates important information for the business

4.6 IMPLEMENTATION

Before you implement CSI you must make sure that:
- the roles for trend analysis, reporting and decision-making are defined (see also the Section 'Organization')
- there is a testing and reporting system with the corresponding technology
- processes are complied with
- services are evaluated internally before the D&I organization discusses the test results with the business
- there is a system for the communication of goals and improvements

The strategic level has the initiative in this. Careful communication is important to prevent visions and goals being warped as one level passes it to another level. The success of CSI depends on the operational level. Give this level enough attention. Make a communication plan that always states the messenger, target group, message, medium, date, frequency and status.

CSI can be implemented through various approaches:

> **service approach** - with this you define the problems with certain services; you create an action plan with the owner of the service: how are we going to remove the problem?
> **lifecycle approach** - with this you look at the results of the various lifecycle phases and you look for possible improvements
> **functional approach** - if many incidents occur with one specific function in an organization, for example in the server group, you can remove as many problems in this function group as possible with a test project

See also 'Basic concepts': Organizational Change and the P-D-C-A Cycle.

Business case

The business case must make it clear whether it is useful to start with CSI. It must indicate what exactly will change in the intended future situation with respect to the starting situation. On the basis of a set **baseline** an organization can estimate what the present situation provides and costs, and how much the improvement of the situation will provide and cost. Formulate this in the language that the business understands. In any case answer the following questions:

> **Where are we?** - determine the present service levels
> **What do we want?** - determine the company vision, mission, goals and objectives
> **What do we need?** - determine what services are essential for the fulfillment of the mission and set priorities on the basis of this
> **What can we pay?** - with the help of service level management (SLM) and financial management, set the budget for D&I Services and see what actions are feasible
> **What do we get for it?** - determine the required results together with the business
> **What have we gotten?** - have Service Operation monitor the service levels and report on them

> **Does it still meet our needs?** - look at further possible improvements with the business

Answer these questions by testing. In the Section 'Processes and other activities' testing is discussed in detail.

For a business case, it is important to have an overview of the **costs** and benefits of CSI. Extra information about the measurement and estimation of costs and benefits can be found in the Section 'Processes and other activities' and in 'Methods, techniques and tools'.

COSTS

When deciding on an improvement initiative, always keep an eye on the costs of introduction, production and maintenance. Examples of this are:

> labor costs
> training costs
> tools to process measurement data
> assessments or benchmark studies
> management time to follow progress
> communication campaigns to create awareness and to change the culture

BENEFITS

Results of a service improvement plan can be divided into:

> **improvements** - measurable improvements with respect to the starting situation
> **benefits** - profit that is the result of improvements (usually in financial terms)
> **Return on Investment (ROI)** - the difference between the costs and benefits of the improvement. Remember to include the risk management (insurance) costs.

› **Value on Investment (VOI)** - ROI, plus the extra value that cannot be expressed in money or that only becomes clear in the long-term; it is difficult to quantify extra value such as higher customer satisfaction; if there are enough 'hard numbers', it still does not add much; a narrative appendix as to this qualitative value is more useful

Define both direct and indirect benefits and consider each group of stakeholders for each organizational level. Define the benefits such that they are measurable. Put the business first. Added value for the business can mean:

› shorter time to market
› customer bonding
› lower maintenance costs for the inventory
› larger market share

CSI can provide the following benefits:

to the business:

› more reliable support for business processes through incident, problem and change management
› higher productivity through increased quality and availability of D&I Services
› the business knows what they can expect of the D&I department and what the D&I department expects of them
› procedures to ensure the continuity of D&I Service are oriented to the needs of the business
› better management information about business processes and D&I Services
› the D&I department has more knowledge of the business processes, so that it can respond better to the desires of the business
› quality projects, releases and changes run according to plan and provide the agreed quality at the agreed costs
› minimal number of unused opportunities
› better relationship between the business and D&I
› higher customer satisfaction

financial:
- efficient D&I Services
- cost effective D&I infrastructure and services
- cost reduction, for example though lower costs for the implementation of changes and less excess processes and equipment
- changes have less (financial) impact on the business
- services meet the requirements but do not overperform
- better division of resources, such that expenditures for the continuity of D&I Services are in proportion with the importance of the business processes that they support
- cost structure is tuned to business needs
- minimal costs and risks with checks that legislation is followed

innovative:
- more proactive development of technology and services through better information on the areas in which changes can lead to profits
- the D&I department reacts better to changes in demands from the business or the market and to new trends
- a business who trusts his D&I supplier dares to 'think big'

internal benefits for the D&I organization:
- more competent D&I department, less chance of errors
- integration of people and processes
- more communication and teamwork (also with the business)
- more productive and more motivated staff
- defined roles and responsibilities
- more effective processes, better use of resources
- D&I repeats and increases profit points through increased process maturity
- better metrics and management reports through structured approach to measurement and knowledge gathering
- better picture of and more trust in present and future D&I improvement opportunities
- services and systems achieve feasible goals within a realistic schedule

- better direction of suppliers
- better relationship with the business
- cost alignment with business needs

Critical Success Factors

A **Critical Success Factor** is a necessary condition for a good result of a service or process. Critical Success Factors for CSI are:

- appoint a **CSI manager** (see also 'Organization')
- adoption by the whole organization
- constant visible management participation in CSI activities, for example by creating a vision and communicating about it
- clear criteria for the prioritization of improvement projects
- adoption of the service cycle approach
- good division of resources
- technology to support improvement activities
- embrace service management processes and do not adapt to meet personal agendas

Challenges and risks

Introduction of CSI comes with the following challenges and risks:

- lack of involvement and action from the management
- poor relationship and communication between D&I and the business
- too little knowledge of the D&I impact on the business and its important processes
- too little knowledge of the business' priorities
- lack of information, monitoring and measurement
- not using the information from reports
- insufficient resources, budget and time
- immature service management processes
- too little or no knowledge management (see also 'Organization')

- trying to change everything at once
- resistance against (cultural) changes
- not enough business or D&I objectives, strategies and policy
- poor supplier management
- not testing
- tooling is too complex or too few
- difference in used technology

Interfaces

CSI uses a lot of data from the entire lifecycle of a service. The information that results from this, together with the demands of the business, the technical specifications, the opportunities of D&I, the budget, trends and legislation, gives insight into the opportunities for the improvement of an organization.

Service Level Management (SLM)

Service level management is the most important process for CSI: it discusses with the business what the D&I organization needs to measure and what the results should be. That is why this section begins with information on what SLM and CSI have in common. For more information about the service level management process see the Section about 'Service Design'.

After each phase of the lifecycle, test whether the improvement initiative has met its goals. This can be done using the **Post Implementation Review** (PIR) from the Change management process.

Because steps 1 and 2 of the CSI improvement process lie primarily with SLM and CSI, an overview of the common ground between CSI and the other ISO-30415 processes and the different Service Lifecycle phases is given starting from step 3 only. Service Operation also provides information about what can be measured before step 2.

In the light of CSI, the objective of SLM is to maintain and improve the quality of D&I Services. SLM does this by making a constant cycle of agreements, monitoring and reporting about D&I Service levels.

In the CSI improvement process, SLM plays a role with:

- What you should measure:
  - consult with the business as to what it would like
- What you can measure:
  - see what has already been measured
  - determine what can and should be measured (SLA, OLAs and Underpinning Contracts)
- Data gathering (measurement):
  - determine what happens with the data: who receives them, what analyses are needed?
- Data processing:
  - evaluate the processed data from the business perspective
  - consider how often the data must be processed and how often they must be reported on
- Data analysis:
  - compare the Service Level Achievements (performance, results) with the SLAs
  - identify and record trends to expose possible patterns
  - determine the need for SIPs
  - the need to adjust existing OLAs or Underpinning Contracts (UCs)
- Presenting the information:
  - reporting to and communicating with the business
  - organizing internal and external service evaluations
  - helping to prioritize activities
- Implementing corrective actions:
  - together with problem and availability management, set up an SIP and ensure that the organization carries out this plan

In this way SLM determines what the organization measures and monitors together with the business, it reports on the performance and signals new business demands. Using this information CSI identifies and prioritizes improvement opportunities. This is the most important input for the SIP (Figure 4.12).

It is recommended that an annual budget is set for SIPs. SLM and CSI can then take quick action, which leads to a proactive attitude.

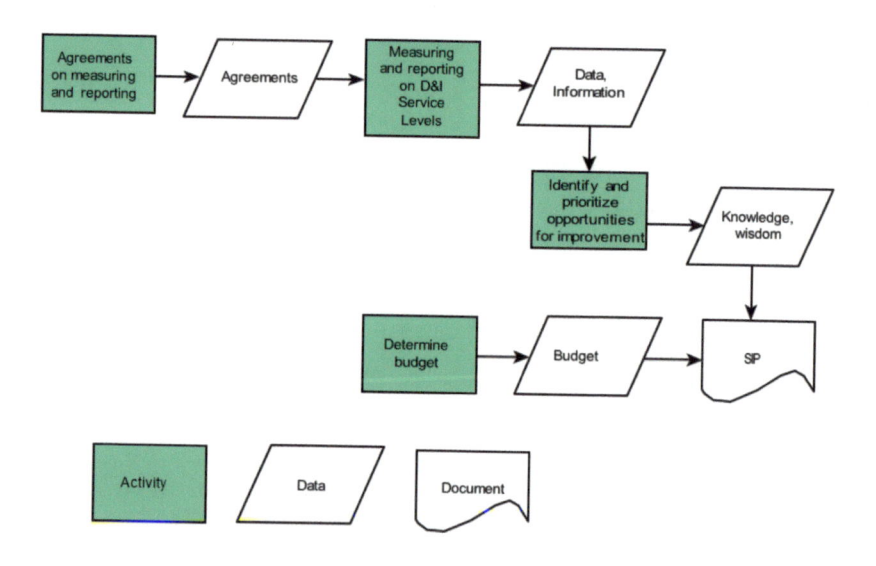

Figure 4.12 SLM and SIP

If an organization outsources its Service Delivery processes, it must also negotiate regarding CSI and include this in the SLA. Otherwise the acting party will no longer be motivated to deliver more than is agreed upon in the contract.

Monitor and gather data (measurement, step 3)

In the Service Lifecycle, Service Strategy monitors the effect of strategies, standards, policy and design decisions.

Service Design monitors and collects information related to the design and modification of services and service management processes. This phase also tests whether the CSFs and KPIs agreed upon with the business are measurable and effective. They also determine what should be measured and set schedules and milestones for this.

Service Transition monitors and measures data about the actual usage of services and service management processes. It develops the monitoring procedures and sets measurement criteria for after implementation.

Service Operation measures the performance of the services and components in the production environment. Once again this forms input for the CSI improvement process: what can be measured and what do these data say?

Apart from SLM, availability management also plays an important role in step 3. This process:

> creates metrics in consultation with the business to measure availability
> determines which tools are needed to make these measurements
> monitors and measures the performance of the infrastructure and frees up enough resources for this
> provides data to CSI
> updates availability plans

Capacity management also undertakes these actions; it does this in order to measure whether the D&I organization can provide the requested services. This can be done from three perspectives:

> **business capacity management** - answers the question 'what do we need?' and 'how to we measure that?' together with the business
> **service capacity management** - answers the question 'what do we need?' from the service perspective and provides information about this to CSI

> **component capacity management** - looks at the components a service is built up of and what needs to be measured to monitor this in its entirety

Incident management defines monitoring requirements to track events and incidents, preferably automated, before they cause problems. It also monitors the reaction, repair, and resolution time and the number of escalations. For example, the D&I Service Desk monitors the number of reports, the average response time and the percentage of callers who hang up prematurely.

Security management monitors and measures the security and records security incidents and problems.

And, finally, financial management monitors and measures the costs and keeps an eye on the budget. It also contributes to the reports as to the costs and ROI of improvement initiatives.

Process data (step 4)

Service Operation processes the data in logical groups. Within these groups availability management and capacity management process the data at the component level regarding availability and capacity. They work together with SLM to give these data an 'end-to-end' perspective and use the agreed upon reporting form to do this.

Incident management and D&I Service Desk check and process data about incidents and Service Requests, and the KPIs related to this. Security management checks and processes data about security incidents and reports on them.

Analyze data (step 5)

Service Strategy analyzes trends, looks at whether the strategies, policy and standards introduced achieve their goal, and whether there are opportunities for improvement. Service Design analyzes the results of design and project activities, and researches trends and opportunities for improvement. It also looks at whether the CSFs and KPIs set in step 2 are still adequate. Service Operation also analyzes results, trends and opportunities for improvement.

The most important Service Operation process for CSI is problem management. This process finds the underlying causes of problems, and these form important opportunities for improvement.

Availability management analyzes performance and trends about component and service data. It compares data with earlier months, quarters and years. It also looks at whether the correct information is being measured and whether SIPs are needed. It uses the following techniques:

> **Component Failure Impact Analysis (CFIA)** - an availability matrix updates which components are strategically important for each service and what role they play (Figure 4.13); a well-arranged configuration management database (CMDB) is necessary for this and can be corded for job function, not personnel name.
> **Fault Tree Analysis (FTA)** - determines the chain of events that can lead to the failure of an D&I Service by the Service Owner (Figure 4.14), reference Figure 4.8.
> **Service Failure Analysis (SFA)** - looks at what a failure means for the business (impact) and what the business expects and aims at end-to-end availability improvement; on the basis

I 147

Configuration Item:	Service A	Service B	
Data Extraction #1	B	B	
Data Extraction #2		B	
Training #1	B	B	
Training #2		B	
ERG #1	X	X	
ERG #2		X	
Team Building	X	X	
Outing	X	X	
External Comms	X	X	
Chamber #1	X	X	
Trade Association #1	X	X	X = Fault means service is unavailable
Chamber #2	A	A	
Training #3	B	B	A = Failsafe configuration
System software #1	B	B	
Data Extraction #3	B	B	B = Failsafe, with changeover time
Chamber #3	X	X	
Figure 4.13 CFIA matrix			"" = No impact

Figure 4.13 CFIA matrix

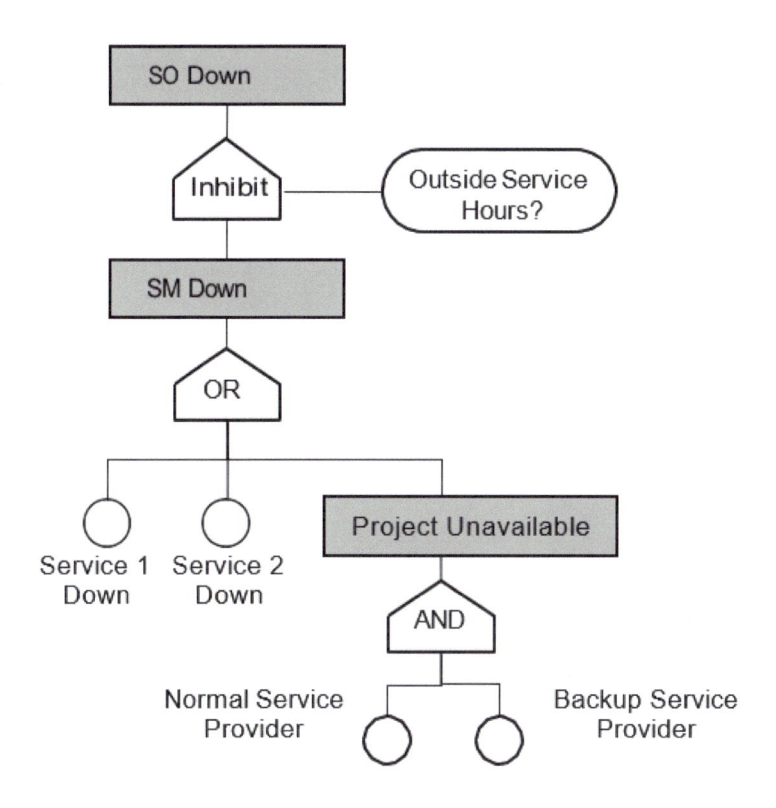

Figure 4.14 Fault Tree Analysis by SO (Service-Owner) & SM (Service Manager)

> **Technical Observation Post (TOP)** - a meeting of D&I personnel with different specializations to discuss one aspect of availability
> **Expanded Incident Lifecycle** - calculates the mean time to restore a service (MTRS); see also the Section on 'maintainability' under Service Strategy

Capacity management analyzes when which customer uses what services, how they use them and how this influences the performance of one or more systems or components. This again provides improvement opportunities to CSI.

Where problem management is oriented toward resolving problems that have already occurred in the past, capacity management tries to prevent problems proactively, by making extra storage capacity ready on time, for example. Often this is done by reproducing the situation in a model, and then asking a number of 'what if' questions.

Incident management and the D&I Service Desk can compare the collected data with earlier results and the agreed service levels. They can also propose SIPs or corrective actions.

Security management uses all the other processes to find the origin of security incidents and problems. It looks for trends and possible improvements in the area of monitoring and looks at whether security strategies produce the intended results.

Every improvement initiative must consult D&I Service Continuity Management (DISCM) to make sure that the D&I Services are not put at risk. **Risk management** plays a central role in this. It analyzes what effects an improvement can have, while in turn CSI analyzes the results of risk management activities, to discover opportunities for improvement. See also Service Design regarding risk management.

Present and use (step 6)

Service Strategy presents results, trends and recommendations for the improvement of adopted strategies, policy and standards. Service Design does this for design improvements and project activities and Service Transition and Service Operation for service and service management processes.

Availability management, capacity management, incident management, D&I Service Desk, problem management, and security management help with making reports and prioritizing corrective actions.

Knowledge management is very important in presenting and using the information for CSI. This is the only way CSI can get a good overview of the knowledge of the organization and the opportunities for improvement. It is also important in order to ensure continual improvement and that all the knowledge and experience gathered is shared and stored. For more information about knowledge management see also the Section about 'Service Transition'.

Implement corrective actions (step 7)

Availability management, capacity management, incident management, D&I Service Desk, problem management and security management perform incremental or corrective actions where approval from the business is not required.

Capacity management can also proceed by introducing **demand management** measures to influence the behavior of the end user:

> - calculation of costs
> - making policy for the proper use of the services
> - communicating expectations
> - education about proper use
> - negotiating maintenance times
> - setting use restrictions, such as limiting the amount of storage space

As with all other changes in the lifecycle, CSI changes must go through the change, release, and deployment process. CSI must therefore submit a Request for Change (RFC) with change management and conduct a PIR after implementation. Also consider the updating of the CMDB by means of configuration management. After this, D&I Service Continuity Management (DISCM) must keep the continuity plan up-to-date.

Finally

The introduction of CSI is not simple. It requires conscious striving toward continual improvement as part of the culture and behavior, and a proactive attitude. In a world where the technology changes very quickly, such a proactive attitude is a big challenge; after all we are constantly controlled by the changes. In a situation of increasing outsourcing and professional development of D&I Service Management, service quality is progressively becoming a distinguishing factor. To get 'in control' and to achieve the desired quality it is preferable to work proactively. CSI is essential to this.

As with many other domains, a step-by-step approach is needed for this. Do not start with a mass approach with all the processes at once, but first determine the biggest problem areas (for example with SWOT) and choose a well-considered approach for the improvements. Recognizing the Critical Success Factors is very important here.

CHAPTER 5
FUNCTIONS AND PROCESSES IN SERVICE OPERATION

5.1 EVENT MANAGEMENT

Introduction

DISM defines an event as follows:

> An **event** *is a random measurable or observable event that has meaning for the management of the D&I infrastructure or delivery of an D&I Service, as well as for the evaluation of the impact that a deviation may have on the service.*

Events are generally registered by a monitoring tool. To ensure effective Service Operations, an organization must be aware of the status of its infrastructure and be able to detect deviations from the regular or expected execution. Good monitoring and control systems provide information.

The **objective** of event management is to detect events, analyze them and determine the right management action. It is the starting point for a great many Service Operation processes and activities.

SCOPE

Event management can be applied to every aspect of service management that requires control and can be automated. Think, for instance, of configuration items, security and environmental factors (eg tracing fire and smoke).

BUSINESS VALUE

Event management generally has indirect value. Some examples of added value for the business:

> - event management provides mechanisms for early detection of incidents
> - event management can ensure that certain automated activities are monitored by exception
> - if event management is integrated into other service management processes, it may detect status changes or exceptions; this allows the right person or team to respond more quickly, thereby improving the process performance
> - event management provides a basis for automated operations; this improves effectiveness and frees up costly human resources for more innovative work

BASIC CONCEPTS

There are many different event types, such as:

> - events that indicate a normal operation, such as a user logging on to use an application

› events that indicate an abnormal operation, such as a user who is trying to log on to an application with an incorrect password or a PC scan that reveals the installation of unauthorized software

› events that signal an unusual but not exceptional operation; it may provide an indication that the situation requires a little more supervision For example utilization of a server's memory reaches within five per cent of its highest acceptable level.

Activities, methods and techniques

The diagram in Figure 5.1 reflects the flow of event management. Use it mainly as a reference, rather than as a factual representation of event management.

The main activities of the event management process are:

› **an event occurs** - events occur all the time, but they are not all detected or registered; it is therefore important for everyone who develops, designs, manages and supports D&I Services and D&I infrastructure to understand what event types must be detected

› **event reporting** - most CIs are designed in such a way that they communicate specific information about themselves in one of the following ways:
  - a management tool probes a device and collects specific data; this is also called 'polling'
  - the CI generates a report if certain conditions are met

› **event detection** - a management tool or agent detects an event report and reads and interprets it

› **event filtering** - decides whether or not the event is communicated to a management tool; if not, the device registers the event in a log file and refrains from taking any further action

› **the significance of events (event classification)** - an organization often uses its own classification to establish the importance of an event, but it is useful to use at least the following three broad categories:
  - *informative* - an event that does not require action and is not an exception, eg a user logging into an application; is

generally stored in the system or service log files and saved for a certain period

- *alert* - occurs when a service or device reaches a threshold; warns the specified person, process or tool to enable it to bring the situation under control and take the required action to prevent an exception; an example of an alert: memory capacity usage on a server is currently at 65% and increasing; if it reaches 75%, the response times are too long and it exceeds the OLA

- *Exception* - means that a service or device is behaving abnormally and a failure to comply with an OLA or SLA; examples of exceptions are:
    - a server is down
    - the response time of a standard transaction over a network exceeds 15 seconds
    - part of the network does not respond to routine queries

> **event correlation** - establishes the significance of an event and determines what actions should be taken

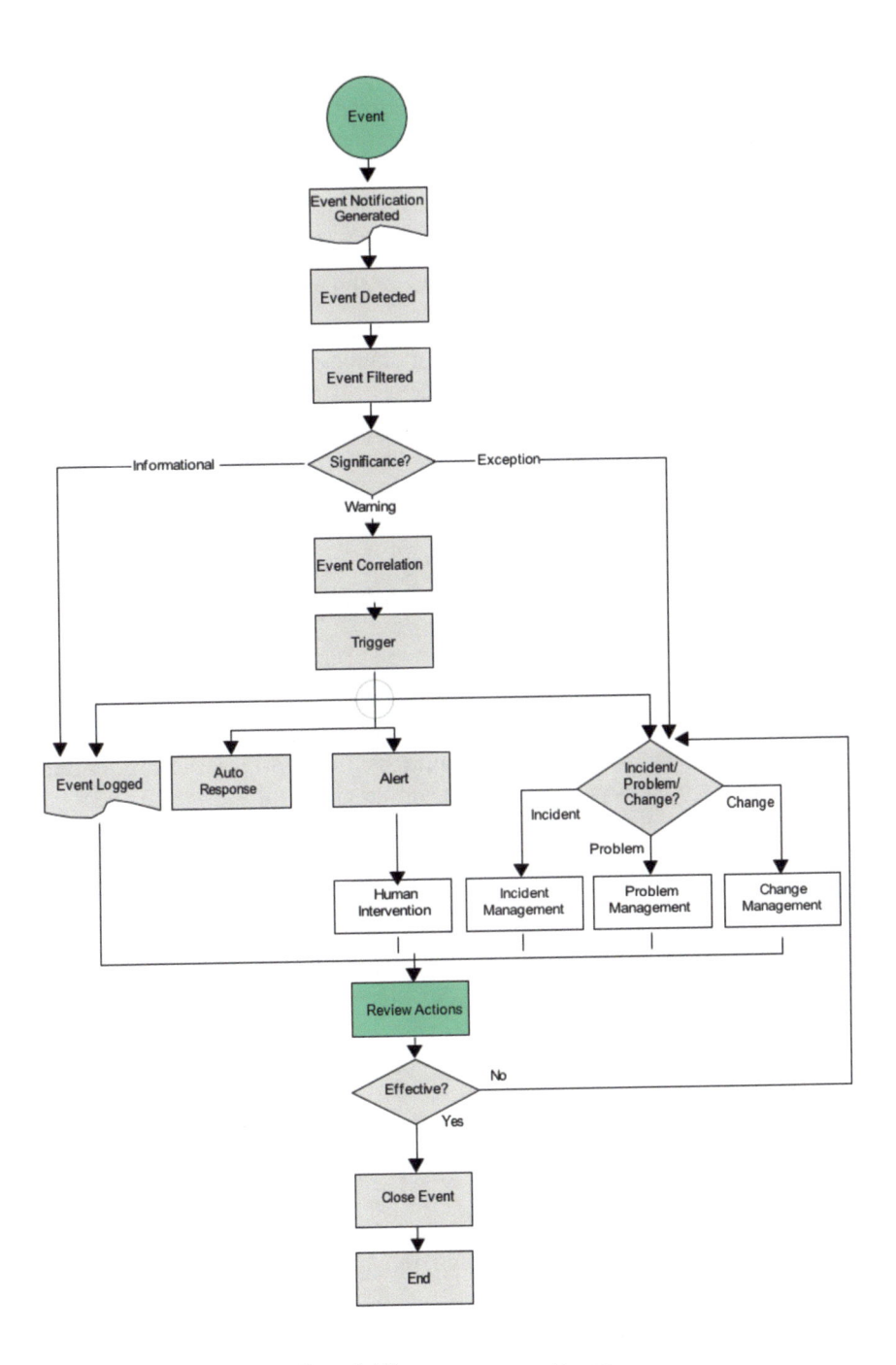

Figure 5.1 The event management process

- **trigger** - if the event is recognized a response is required; the mechanism that initiates that response is called a trigger; there are different trigger types, including:
  - *incident triggers* generate a record in the incident management system, thereby starting up the incident management process
  - *scripts* execute specific actions, such as rebooting a device
  - *database triggers* deny a user access to specific records or fields, or create and delete entries in a database
- **response options** - the process provides a number of response options, a combination of which are allowed:
  - event logging
  - automatic response
  - alert and human intervention
  - submitting a *Request for Change (RFC)*
  - opening an incident record
  - opening a link to a problem record
- **assessment actions** - thousands of events are generated every day, which makes it impossible to assess each individual event formally; however, you should check all important events or exceptions to determine whether they have been treated correctly, or whether event types are counted; in many cases this can be done automatically
- **closing the event** - some events remain open until specific actions have been taken, eg an event linked to an open incident

Interfaces

Every event type is able to **trigger** event management. You should determine what events are important and require action. Triggers consists of, among other things:

- exceptions at every level of CI performance established in the design
- specifications, Operational Level Agreements or standard processing procedures
- an exception in a business process that is monitored by event management

> a status change in a device or database record

Event management has **interfaces** with every process that requires monitoring and control. The most important are incident, problem and change management. In addition, configuration management can use events to determine the current status of a CI in the infrastructure. Finally, events represent a rich source of information for knowledge management systems.

Metrics

Metrics are required for every measuring period, to verify the effectiveness and efficiency of the event management process, eg

> **number of** events per category
> number of important events
> number and percentage of events requiring human intervention, and in how many cases this occurred
> the number and percentage of events that resulted in incidents and changes
> the number and percentage of each event type per platform or application

Implementation

The main **risks** are:

> being unable to realize sufficient funds
> establishing the right level of filtering
> being unable to maintain momentum during rollout of the required *monitoring agents*

DESIGNING FOR EVENT MANAGEMENT

Event management constitutes the basis for monitoring the performance and availability of a service. This is why availability and capacity management must specify and agree on the precise monitoring targets and mechanisms. Various instruments exist for this purpose:

> **instrumentation** - defines how best to monitor and manage the D&I infrastructure and D&I Services, and creates an appropriate design Determine:
> - what needs to be monitored
> - what monitoring type is required (active or passive, performance or output)
> - when the monitoring should generate an event
> -
> - You should also design a number of mechanisms to:
> - generate events
> - select data and use them for event records
> - log and save events
>
> **error messages** - important for all components (hardware, software, networks, etc); design all software applications in such a way that they can support event management, eg by means of practical error messages or codes that clearly indicate what is going wrong where and the causes
>
> **event detection and alert mechanisms** - for a good design, you need the following:
> - detailed knowledge of the Service Level Requirements of the service that is supported by every CI
> - information on who will support the CI
> - knowledge of the normal and abnormal state of affairs for the CI
> - information that can help determine problems with CIs

5.2 INCIDENT MANAGEMENT

INTRODUCTION

The incident management process handles all incidents. These may be failures, questions or queries that are reported by personnel both internal or external to the organization, or that are automatically detected through sensors that are identifiable from events.

DISM for ISO-30415 defines an incident as:

> An **incident** is an unplanned interruption to an D&I Service or reduction in the quality of an D&I Service. Failure of a CI that has not yet affected service is also an incident.

The main objective of the incident management process is to resume the regular state of affairs as quickly as possible and minimize the impact on business processes.

SCOPE

Incident management covers every event that disrupts or might disrupt a service. This means that it includes events reported directly by users, either via the D&I Service Desk or various tools.

Incidents can also be reported or logged by technical staff, which does not necessarily mean that every event is an incident.

While incidents and *service requests* are both reported to the D&I Service Desk, they are not the same thing. *service requests* are not service disruptions but user requests for support, delivery, information, advice or documentation.

BUSINESS VALUE

The value of incident management includes:

> the possibility to track and solve incidents results in reduced downtime for the business; as a result the service is available for longer

> the possibility to align D&I operations with the business priorities; the reason is that incident management is able to identify business priorities and distribute resources dynamically

> the possibility to establish potential improvements for services

Incident management is clearly visible to the business, meaning that its value is easier to demonstrate than for other areas in Service Operations. For this reason, it is one of the first processes to be implemented in service management projects.

BASIC CONCEPTS

The following elements should be taken into account in incident management:

> **time limits** - agree on time limits for all phases and use them as targets in Operational Level Agreements (OLAs) and Underpinning Contracts (UCs)

> **incident models** - an incident model is a way to determine the steps that are necessary to execute a process correctly (in this case, the processing of certain incident types); it means that standard incidents will be handled correctly and within the agreed timeframes

> **major incidents** - a separate procedure is required for major incidents, with shorter timeframes and higher urgency; agree what a major incident is and map the entire incident priority system

People sometimes confuse a major incident with a problem. However, an incident always remains an incident. Its impact or priority may increase, but it never becomes a problem. A problem is the underlying cause of one or more incidents and always remains a separate entity.

Activities, methods and techniques

The incident management process consists of the following steps (Figure 5.2):

1. identification
2. registration
3. classification
4. prioritisation
5. diagnosis
6. escalation
7. investigation and diagnosis
8. resolution and recovery
9. closing

An incident is not handled until it is known to exist. This is called **incident identification.** From a business perspective, it is generally unacceptable to wait until a user experiences the impact of an incident and contacts the D&I Service Desk. The organization must try to monitor all important components, so that failures or potential failures can be detected as early as possible and the incident management process can be initiated. In the perfect situation, incidents are solved before they have an impact on the users.

All incidents must be registered in full, including date and time: **incident registration.** This applies to incidents received via the D&I Service Desk as well as those that are detected automatically via an event warning system. Register all relevant information relating to the nature of the incident to ensure a complete historical record. If the incident is transferred to other support groups, they will have all of the relevant information at their disposal. You should at least record:

> a unique reference number
> incident category
> incident urgency

- incident priority
- name/ID of the person and/or group who registered the incident
- description of symptoms
- activities undertaken to solve the incident

Use an appropriate **incident classification** coding for registration to record the precise call type. This is important at a later stage when incident types and frequencies are analyzed, to establish trends that can be used for problem management, provider management and other DISM activities.

When registering an incident, it is possible that the available data are incomplete, misleading or incorrect. It is therefore important to check the classification of the incident and update it while

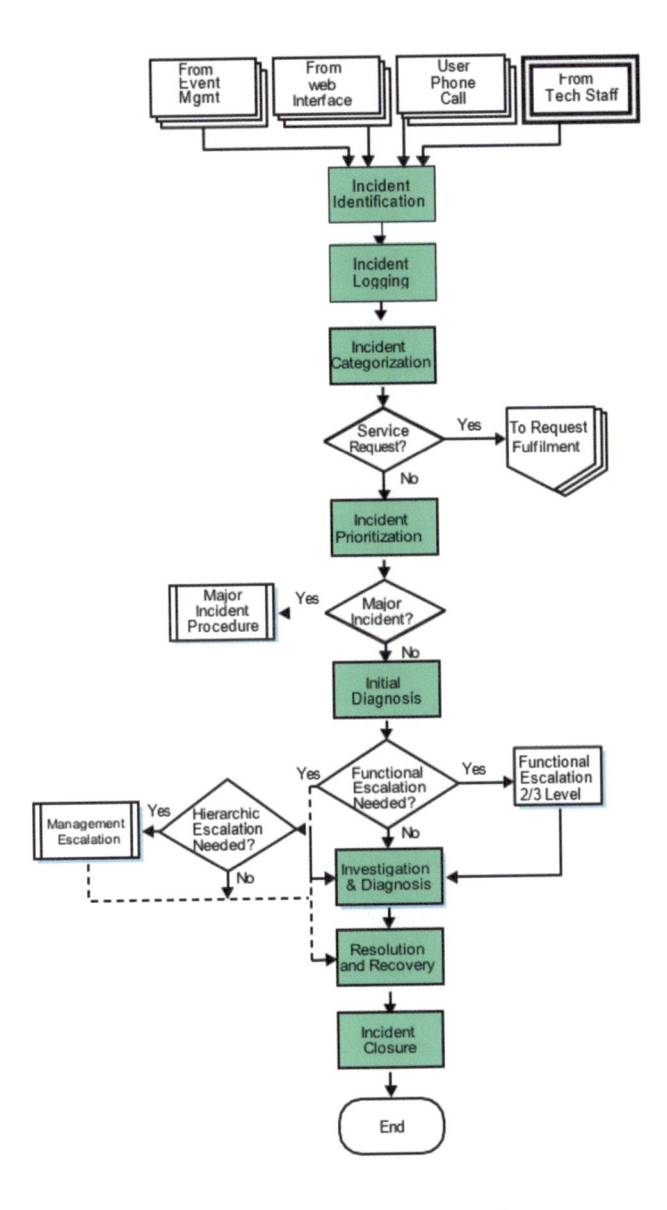

Figure 5.2 The incident management diagram

concluding a call. An example of a categorized incident is: software, application, finance suite and purchase order system.

Another important aspect of registering every incident is to allocate the right **priority** code. Support agents and tools use this code to determine how they should handle the incident.

The priority of an incident can usually be determined by establishing its urgency (how fast does the business need a solution) and impact. The number of users touched by an incident is often an indication of its impact.

When a user reports an incident via the D&I Service Desk, the D&I Service Desk agent must try to record the greatest possible number of symptoms of the incident in terms of a first **diagnosis**. He also tries to establish what went wrong and how it should be corrected. Diagnostic scripts and *known error* information can be very useful in this context. If possible, the help desk agent solves the incident immediately and closes the incident.

If this is impossible, he *escalates* the incident.

This can be achieved in two ways:

> **functional escalation** - if it is clear that the D&I Service Desk cannot solve the incident (quickly enough), it must be escalated immediately for further support; if the organization has a second line support group and the D&I Service Desk believes that they can solve the incident, it forwards the incident to the second line; if it is clear that more technical knowledge is required for the incident and the second line support is unable to solve the incident within the agreed timeframe, it must be escalated to the third line support group

> **hierarchical escalation** - the relevant D&I managers must be warned in the event of more serious incidents (eg priority 1 incidents); hierarchical escalation is also used if there are inadequate resources to solve the incident; hierarchical escalation means that the organization calls upon the management higher up in the chain; senior managers are aware of the incident and can take the required steps, such as allocating additional resources or calling upon suppliers

When handling an incident, each support group **investigates** what went wrong. It also makes a **diagnosis**. Document all these activities in the incident record to ensure that a complete overview of all activities is available.

In case of incidents where the user is only looking for information, the D&I Service Desk must be able to provide the answer quickly and solve the *service request*.

If a possible solution has been determined, it must be implemented and tested: Solution and recovery. The following actions can then be taken:

> ask the user to perform specific operations on his desktop
> the D&I Service Desk can execute the solution centrally or use remote software to take control of the user's computer and implement a solution
> ask a supplier to solve the error

The support group returns the incident to the D&I Service Desk, which **closes the incident.** However, it first checks that the incident has been solved and that the users are satisfied with the solution. It must also close the classification, check that the user is satisfied, update the incident documentation, determine whether the incident could recur, and decide whether action should be taken to prevent this. The incident can then be formally closed.

INFORMATION MANAGEMENT

Most information used by incident management is provided by incident management tools and incident records. Incident management also has access to the configuration management system (CMS). This makes it possible to identify the CIs touched by the incident. The impact of the incident can also be assessed.

Interfaces

Incidents can be **triggered** in many ways. The most common route is via a user who calls the D&I Service Desk or completes an incident registration

| 167

form via the internet. However, many incidents are registered more and more often by event management tools.

The processes below have **interfaces** with incident management:

> **Problem management** - Incidents are often caused by underlying problems that must be solved to prevent the incident from recurring. Incident management offers a place to report these problems.
> **Configuration management** - Configuration management provides the data used to identify and track incidents. The configuration management system (CMS) is used, among other things, to identify defective components and determine the impact of an incident. The CMS is also used to identify the users who are impacted by potential problems.
> **Change management** - If a change is necessary to implement a workaround or solution, it is registered as an RFC and executed by change management. Incident management is able to track and solve incidents resulting from inappropriate changes.
> **Capacity management** - Incident management triggers performance monitoring if a performance problem occurs. Capacity management can offer workarounds for incidents.
> **Availability management** - Availability management uses data from incident management to determine the availability of D&I Services, and establishes where the incident lifecycle can be improved.
> **Service level management (SLM)** - SLM monitors the agreements with customers concerning the support to be provided. Incident management reports to SLM. This process, for instance, can evaluate SLAs objectively and regularly. SLM establish acceptable service levels within which incident management must work.

Metrics

Metrics make it possible to assess the effectiveness, efficiency and operation of the incident management process. Examples of metrics are:

> the total number of incidents
> the number and percentage of major incidents

- the average cost per incident
- the number and percentage of incorrectly allocated incidents
- the percentage of incidents handled within the agreed timeframe

Implementation

Incident management has the following challenges:

- to detect incidents as quickly as possible
- to convince all staff (both technical teams and users) that all incidents must be registered and encourage them to use web-based options to solve incidents themselves
- the availability of information about problems and known errors, enabling incident management staff to learn from previous incidents and track the status of solutions
- integration with the configuration management system to determine the relationship between CIs and refer to the history of CIs when providing first line support
- integration with the service level management process; this helps incident management to determine the impact and priority of incidents correctly and to define and execute escalation procedures

The following **Critical Success Factors** (CSFs) are vital to successful incident management:

- a good D&I Service Desk
- clearly defined SLA targets
- adequate support staff that is customer-oriented and technically qualified, and possesses the right competencies at all process levels
- integrated support tools to control and manage the process
- OLAs and UCs to influence and shape the behavior of all support personnel

Risks for successful incident management are:

- being overwhelmed by incidents that cannot be handled within an acceptable timeframe due to lack of well-trained resources

> incidents that make no progress because inadequate support tools fail to give warning or report progress
> lack of adequate information sources due to unsuitable tools or lack of integration
> no coinciding objectives or actions due to unaligned or nonexistent OLAs or UCs

5.3 REQUEST FULFILLMENT

Introduction

ISO-30415 uses the term service request as a general description for the varying requests that users submit to the D&I department.

> *A **service request** is a request from a user for information, advice, a standard change, or access to a service.*

For example, a service request can be a request for a password change or the additional installation of a software application on a certain work station. Because these requests occur on a regular basis and involve little risk, it is better that they are handled in a separate process.

Request fulfillment (implementation of requests) processes service requests from the users. The **objectives** of the request fulfillment process are:

> to offer users a channel through which they can request and receive services; to this effect an agreed approval and qualification process must exist
> to provide users and customers with information about the availability of services and the procedure for obtaining these services
> to supply the components of standard services (for instance, licenses and software media)
> to assist with general information, complaints or comments

SCOPE

The process for handling requests depends on the nature of the request. In most cases the process can be divided into a series of activities that need to be completed. Some organizations treat the service requests as a special type of incident. However, there is an important difference between an incident and a service request. An incident is usually an unplanned event, whereas a service request tends to be something that can and must be planned.

VALUE FOR THE BUSINESS

The value of request fulfillment is the ability to offer fast and effective access to standard services that the business can use to improve the productivity or the quality of the business services and products.

Request fulfillment reduces the amount of 'red tape' in requesting and receiving access to existing or new services. This reduces the cost for the supply of these services.

BASIC CONCEPTS

Many service requests recur on a regular basis. This is why a process flow can be devised in advance, stipulating the phases needed to handle the requests, the individuals or support groups involved, time limits and escalation paths. The service request is usually handled as a standard change.

Activities, working methods and techniques

Request fulfillment consists of the following activities, methods and techniques:

> - **menu selection** - by means of request fulfillment, users can submit their own service request via a link to service management tools; in the ideal situation the user will be offered a menu via a web interface, so that they can select and enter the details of a service request

- **financial authorisation** - most service requests have financial implications; the cost for handling a request must first be determined; it is possible to agree fixed prices for standard requests and give instant authorisation for these requests; in all other cases the cost must first be estimated, after which the user must give permission
- **fulfillment** - the actual fulfillment activity depends on the nature of the service request; the D&I Service Desk can handle simple requests, whereas others must be forwarded to specialist groups or suppliers
- **conclusion** - once the service request has been completed the D&I Service Desk will close off the request

Interfaces

Most requests are **triggered** by a user who rings the D&I Service Desk or a user who completes a request form on-screen. Many service requests come in via the D&I Service Desks and can be handled through the incident management process. Some organizations choose to handle all requests via this route, others prefer a separate process.

There is also a strong **link** between request fulfillment, release management, asset management and configuration management, because some requests deal with the roll-out of new or improved components that can be implemented automatically.

Request fulfillment is dependent on information from the following **sources:**

- service requests
- Requests for Change
- Service Portfolio
- security policy

Metrics

The metrics required to evaluate the efficiency and effectiveness of request fulfillment are:

- the total number of service requests
- the breakdown of service requests by phase
- the size of the current backlog of outstanding service requests
- the average time for handling each type of service request
- the number and percentage of service requests that are handled within the agreed time
- the average cost per type of service request
- the level of customer satisfaction in respect of the handling of service requests

Implementation

Request fulfillment is faced with the following **challenges**:

- to clearly define and document the type of request that is being handled in the request fulfillment process, so that all parties know what the scope is
- to establish front-end options, so that users can make their own link to the request fulfillment process
- Request fulfillment is dependent on the following Critical Success Factors:
- there must be agreement about which services are standardized and who is authorized to request them; there must also be agreement about the cost of these services
- publication of these services for the benefit of the users, as part of the Service Catalogue
- there must be a definition of a standard fulfillment procedure for each service being requested
- there must be a single point of contact for requesting the service; this is often done via the D&I Service Desk or via an internet request, but can also be made via an automated request directly in the request fulfillment procurement system

> self-service tools are needed to offer a front-end interface to users; it is important that this interface can communicate with the back-end fulfillment tools

Request fulfillment has the following **risks:**

> If the scope is ill-defined, people will not know exactly what the process is supposed to handle.
> Poorly designed or implemented user interfaces may make it difficult for users to submit requests.
> Poorly designed or realized back-end fulfillment processes may result in the system being unable to handle the number or type of requests being submitted.
> Insufficient monitoring capacity may result in no accurate metrics being collected.

5.4 PROBLEM MANAGEMENT

Introduction

ISO-30415 defines a problem as follows:

> A **problem** is the unknown cause of one or more incidents.

Problem management is responsible for the control of the lifecycle of all problems. The primary **objective** of problem management is to prevent problems and incidents, eliminate repeating incidents and minimize the impact of incidents that cannot be prevented.

SCOPE

Problem management comprises all the activities needed to diagnose the underlying cause of incidents and to find a solution for these problems. It must also ensure that the solution is implemented via the correct control procedures, in other words through the use of change management and release management.

VALUE FOR THE BUSINESS

Problem management works together with incident management and change management to ensure improvements in the availability and quality of the D&I Service provision. When incidents are resolved the solution is registered. At a given moment this information is used to accelerate the incident handling and identify permanent solutions. This reduces the number of incidents and the handling time, resulting in shorter disruption times and fewer disruptions to the business critical systems.

BASIC CONCEPTS

Many problems are unique and need to be handled separately. However, it is possible that some incidents may occur more than once as a result of underlying problems.

ISO-30415 defines a know-error as:

> A **problem** that has a documented root cause and a work arround.

ISO-30415 defines a workaround as:

> **Workaround**: reducing or eliminating the impact of an incident or problem for which a full resolution is not yet available.

In addition to creating a Known Error Database (KEDB) for faster diagnoses, the creation of a **problem model** for the handling of future problems may be useful. Such a standard model supports with the steps that need to be taken, the responsibilities of people involved and the necessary timescales.

Activities, methods and techniques

Problem management consists of two important processes:

> **reactive problem management** - performed by Service Operation
> **proactive problem management** - initiated by Service Operation, but usually managed by CSI (Continual Service Improvement) (see also Chapter 13)

Reactive problem management consists of the following activities (Figure 5.3):

> identification
> registration
> classification
> prioritisation
> investigation and diagnosis
> decide on workarounds
> identification of known errors
> resolution
> conclusion
> review
> correction of errors found

Identification of problems is carried out using the following methods:

> The D&I Service Desk suspects or identifies an unknown cause of one or more incidents. This results in a problem registration. It may also be clear straightaway that an incident was caused by a major problem. In this case a problem registration takes place immediately.
> Analysis of an incident by the technical support group reveals that there is an underlying problem.
> There is automatic tracing of an infrastructural or application error, whereby event or alert tools automatically create an incident registration that highlights the need for a problem registration.

- The supplier reports a problem that needs to be resolved.
- Analysis of incidents takes place as part of corrective problem management. This results in a problem registration so that the underlying cause can be investigated further.

Analyze incident and problem data on a regular basis in order to identify trends. To this effect an efficient and detailed classification of incidents and problems is required, as well as regular reporting of patterns and problem areas.

Irrespective of the identification method, all details of the problem must be registered (**problem registration**), so that a comprehensive historic report is created. The information must be date and time stamped, so that proper control and escalation are possible.

Problems must be classified in the same way as incidents, so that the true nature of the problem can be established quickly and easily. **Problem classification** provides useful management information.

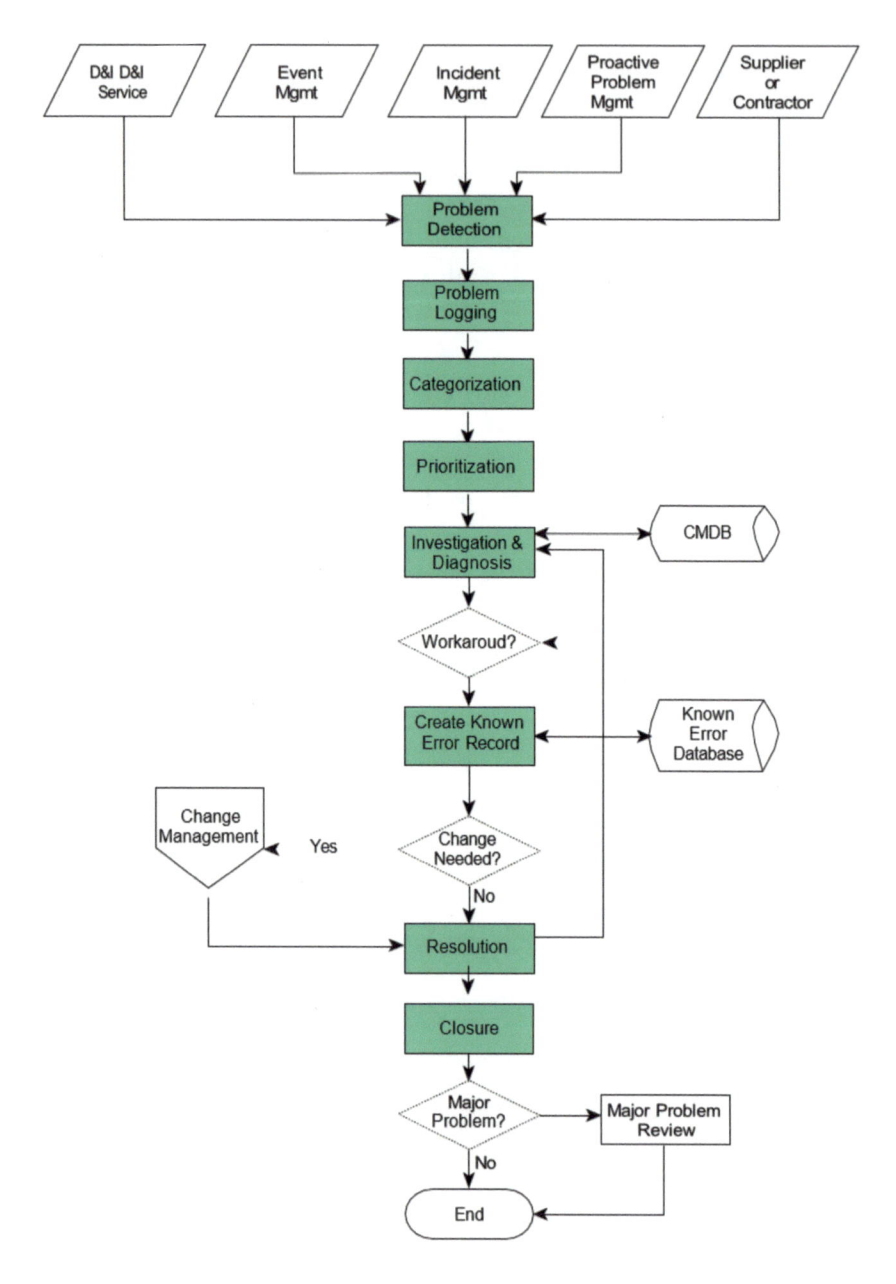

Figure 5.5 Problem management diagram

As is the case for incidents, problems must also be given a priority in the same manner and for the same reasons. In this context also take into account the frequency and impact of the related incidents and the seriousness of the problems. Examples of such considerations are:

> Can the system be repaired or does it need to be replaced?
> What are the costs?
> How many people, and with what expertise are needed to resolve the problem?
> How much time is needed to resolve the problem?
> How big is the problem?

In order to find the underlying cause of the problem and make a **diagnosis**, an **investigation** must be performed. The speed and nature of this investigation depend on the impact, seriousness and urgency of the problem. Use the proper level of resources and expertise to find a solution.

It is often useful to reproduce the problem, so that it becomes clear what went wrong. Next you can use different methods to determine what the best solution is. This is best done by using a test system that reflects production.

Many problem analysis, diagnosis and solution techniques are available, including:

> chronological analysis
> Pain Value Analysis
> Kepner-Tregoe
> brainstorming
> Ishikawa diagrams
> Pareto analysis

In some cases a temporary solution, a **workaround**, is possible for incidents that were caused by a problem. It is important, however, that the problem reporting remains open and that the details about the workaround are included in the problem reporting.

As soon as the diagnosis has been made, and especially if a workaround has been found, the **identified known errors** must be listed in a known error report and placed in the Known Error Database. Should other incidents and problems occur they can be identified and the service can be resumed more quickly.

As soon as a **solution** has been found it should, ideally, be applied to resolve the problem. In reality, there are preventative measures to make sure that the solution does not cause further problems. If a change in functionality is needed a *Request for Change* is required that must follow the steps of the change management process.

If the change has been completed and successfully evaluated and the solution has been applied, the problem report can formerly be **closed off**, as can the related incident reports that are still outstanding. Remember to check whether the report contains a full description of all the events.

After every **major problem** a **review** must be performed to learn lessons for the future. In particular the review must assess:

- what went well
- what went wrong
- what can be done better in future
- how the same problem can be prevented from recurring
- whether a third party is responsible and whether any follow-up actions are needed

It is very rare that new applications, systems or software releases do not contain **errors**. In most cases a priority system is used during testing that removes the most serious errors, but it is possible that minor errors are not corrected.

INFORMATION MANAGEMENT

The *CMS* contains details on all the components of the D&I infrastructure and on the relationship between these components. It is a valuable source for problem diagnosis and for the evaluation of the impact of problems.

The purpose of a **Known Error Database** (KEDB) is to store knowledge about incidents and problems and how they were remedied, so that a quicker diagnosis and solution can be found if further incidents and problems occur.

The known error registration must contain the exact details about the error and the symptoms that occurred, together with the exact details of a workaround or solution that can be implemented to resume the service or resolve the problem.

It may be that there is no business case for a permanent solution for certain problems. For instance, if the problem does not cause serious disruptions, a workaround already exists and the costs of resolving the problem exceed the advantages of a permanent solution, problem management may decide to tolerate the problem.

Like the configuration management system (CMS), the KEDB is part of a larger Service Knowledge Management System (SKMS) (Figure 5.4). The Section on 'Service Transition' (Chapter 11) gives more information about the SKMS.

INTERFACES

The majority of problem registrations are **triggered** as a response to one or more incidents, especially by D&I Service Desk staff. Other problem registrations and corresponding known errors are triggered during testing, especially during so-called user acceptance tests that determine whether a release will proceed despite some known errors.

The following processes **interface** with problem management:

> Service Transition:
- *Change management* - problem management ensures that all solutions and workarounds for which change is necessary are implemented in a CI via an RFC; change management monitors the progress of these changes and keeps problem management informed
- *Configuration management* - problem management uses the CMS to identify wrong CIs and to determine the impact of problems and solutions
- *Release and deployment management* - is responsible for the rollout of problem fixes in a production environment

> Service Design:
- *Availability management* - helps determine how the disruption time can be minimized and how the production time (*uptime*) can be increased; a lot of the management information in problem management is passed on to availability management
- *Capacity management* - ensures the optimum use of resources and provides problem management with important information such as capacity registrations and performance matters; capacity management also supports the application of corrective measures
- *D&I Service Continuity Management (DISCM)* - problem management acts as a starting point for DISCM: a problem is not resolved if it does not have an important impact on the business

> Continual Service Improvement:
- *Service level management* - incidents and problems influence the quality of D&I Services provided by SLM; problem management contributes to improving service levels and the management information provided by it is used as the basis for some SLA review components

> Service Strategy:
> - Financial management – problem management provides management information about the cost of resolving and preventing problems; in this way the information can be used as input for budgeting and accounting systems and Total Cost of Ownership calculations

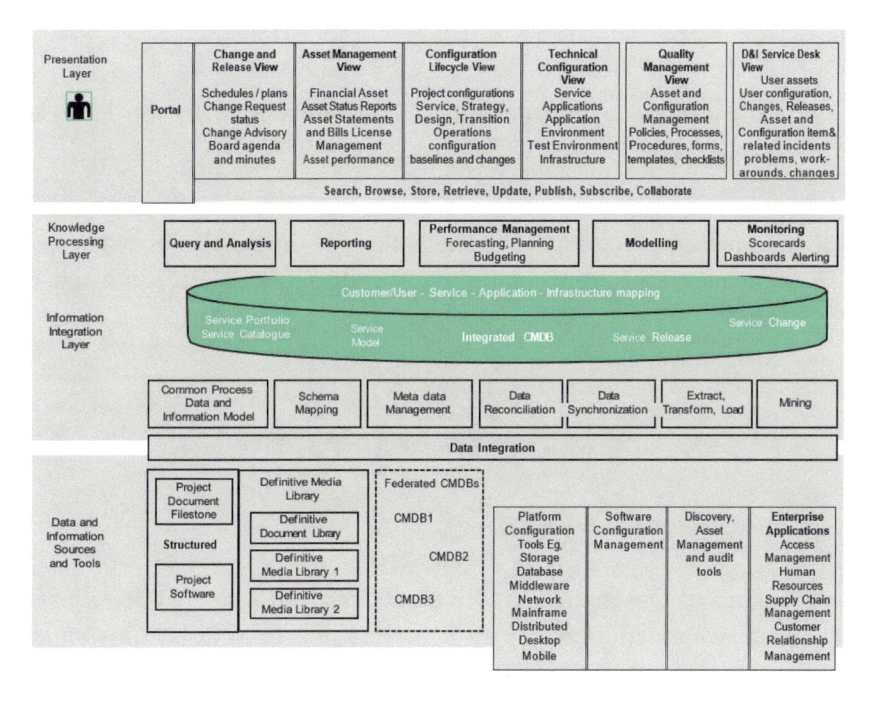

Figure 5.4 delivery layers

Metrics

The following metrics are used to evaluate the efficiency, effectiveness and implementation of the problem management process:

> - the total number of problems that were registered in the period
> - the percentage of problems that were resolved within SLA targets (and the percentage of problems that were not solved)

- the number and percentage of problems for which more time was needed to resolve them
- the backlog of outstanding problems and the trend (static, decreasing, increasing)
- the average costs for handling a problem
- the number of major problems (outstanding, closed and backlog)
- the percentage of successful major problem reviews
- the number of known errors added to the KEDB
- the accuracy percentage of the KEDB (from checks of the database)

Implementation

Problem management is highly dependent on the formulation of an effective incident management process and the use of the proper tools. These help to identify problems as quickly as possible.

5.5 ACCESS MANAGEMENT

Introduction

Access management grants authorized users the right to use a service, but denies unauthorized users access. Some organizations also call it 'rights management' or 'identity management'.

SCOPE

Access management ensures that users have access to a service, but it does not guarantee that access is always available at the agreed times. This is handled by availability management.

Access management can be initiated via a number of mechanisms, such as the D&I Service Desk by means of a service request.

BUSINESS VALUE

Access management has the following value:

- controlled access to services enables the organization to maintain confidentiality of its information more effectively
- staff have the right access level to do their jobs properly
- the risk of errors during data entry or the use of a vital service by an unqualified user is lower
- there is the option to withdraw access rights more easily when it is necessary access may be necessary for compliance (eg SOX, HIPAA, CobiT)

BASIC CONCEPTS

Access management has the following basic concepts:

- **access** - refers to the level and scope of the functionality of a service or data that a user is allowed to use
- **identity** - refers to the information about the persons who the organization distinguish as individuals; establishes their status in the organization
- **rights** (also called privileges) - refers to the actual settings for a user; which service (group) they are allowed to use; typical rights include reading, writing, executing, editing and deleting
- **services or service groups** - most users have access to multiple services; it is therefore more effective to grant every user or group of users access to an entire series of services that they are allowed to use simultaneously
- **directory services** - refers to a specific type of tool used to manage access and rights

Activities, methods and techniques

Access (or limitation of access) can be requested via a number of mechanisms, such as:

> a standard request generated by the human resources department; this generally occurs when someone is hired, promoted or leaves the company
> a *Request for Change* (RFC)
> an RFC submitted via the request fulfillment process
> execution of an authorized script or option

Access management consists of the following activities:

> **verification** - access management must verify every access request for an D&I Service from two perspectives:
> - Is the user requesting access truly the person he says he is?
> - Does the user have a legitimate reason to use the service?
>
> **granting rights** - access management does not decide who gets access to what D&I Services; it only executes the policy and rules defined by Service Strategy and Service Design

The more groups and roles exist, the greater the chance of a role conflict occurring. In this context, role conflicts refer to a situation in which two specific roles or groups allocated to a user can cause trouble due to conflicting interests. One example is that one role requires access while the other forbids it.

> **monitoring identity status** - user roles may vary over time, with an impact on their service needs; examples of what may change a role are: job changes, promotion, dismissal, retirement or death
>
> **registering and monitoring access** - access management does not only respond to requests; it must also ensure that the rights it has granted are used correctly. This is why access monitoring and control must be included in the monitoring activities of all technical and application management functions as well as all Service Operation processes.
>
> **revoking or limiting rights** - in addition to granting rights to use a service, access management is also responsible for withdrawing those rights; but it cannot make the actual decision

INFORMATION MANAGEMENT

The **identity** of a user is the information that distinguishes him as an individual and verifies his status in the organization. The following data may be used, for instance:

- name
- contact details such as phone number and (e-mail) address
- physical documentation, such as driver's license and passport
- numbers referring to a document or entry in a database, such as social security number and driver's license number
- biometric information, such as fingerprints, DNA and voice recognition patterns

While every **user** has a separate identity and every D&I Service can be considered an individual identity, it often makes sense to **group** them for easier management. Sometimes the terms user profile, user template or user role are used to describe this type of grouping.

Most organizations have a standard collection of services for all individual users regardless of their position or job. But some users have a special role. For instance, in addition to the standard services a user may also fulfill a marketing management role for which he needs access to several special marketing and financial modeling tools and data.

Interfaces

Access management is **triggered** by a user's request for access to a service (group). Such a request may originate with:

- an RFC
- a service request
- a request from the Human Resources (HR) department
- a request from a manager or department fulfilling an HR role or who has made a decision to use a service for the first time

Access management has **relationships** with various other processes. Since every access request for a service represents a change, change management plays an important part in controlling the access requests.

Service level management monitors the agreements concerning access to each service. This includes the criteria for who has access to a service, the costs and the access level granted to different types of users.

Access management also has a close relationship with configuration management. The CMS can be used for data storage and be studied to determine the current access details.

Metrics

Metrics used to measure the effectiveness and efficiency of access management are:

> the number of access requests (service requests and RFCs)
> the number of times access has been granted by a service, user or department
> the number of incidents required to reset access rights
> the number of incidents caused by incorrect access settings

Implementation

The **conditions** for successful access management include:

> the possibility to verify a user's identity
> the possibility to verify the identity of the person or entity granting permission
> the possibility to grant several access rights to an individual user
> a database of all users and the rights they have been granted

5.6 MONITORING AND CONTROL

Introduction

The measuring and control of services is based on a continuous cycle of monitoring, reporting and initiating action. We will discuss this cycle in detail because it is essential to the supply, support and improvement of services.

BASIC CONCEPTS

Three terms play a leading role in monitoring and control:

> monitoring
> reporting
> control

Monitoring refers to the observation of a situation to discover changes that occur over time.

Reporting refers to the analysis, production and distribution of the output of the activity that is being monitored.

Control refers to the management of the usefulness or behavior of a device, system or service. There are three conditions for control:

1. the action must ensure that the behavior conforms to a defined standard or norm
2. the conditions leading to the action must be defined, understood and confirmed
3. the action must be defined, approved and suitable for these conditions

Activities, methods and techniques

THE MONITORING/CONTROL CYCLE

The best-known model for the description of control is the monitoring/ control cycle. Although it is a simple model it has many complex applications in D&I Service Management. In this section we describe the basic concepts of the model. Next we will show how important these concepts are for the Service Management Lifecycle. Figure 5.5 reflects the basic principles of control.

This cycle measures an activity and its benefits by means of a pre-defined norm or standard to determine whether the results are within the target values for performance or quality. If this is not the case, action must be taken to improve the situation or resume the normal performance.

There are two types of monitoring/ control cycles:

> **Open cycle systems** - are designed for a specific activity, irrespective of the environmental conditions; making a backup, for instance, can be initiated at a specified moment and be completed regardless of other conditions

> **Closed cycle systems** - monitoring of an environment and responding to changes in this environment; if, in a network, the network transactions exceed a certain number, the control system will redirect the 'traffic' via a backup circuit in order to regulate the network transactions

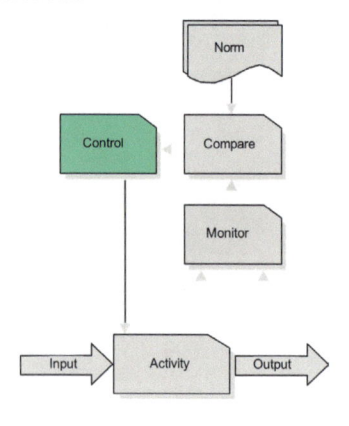

Figure 5.5 The monitoring/control cycle

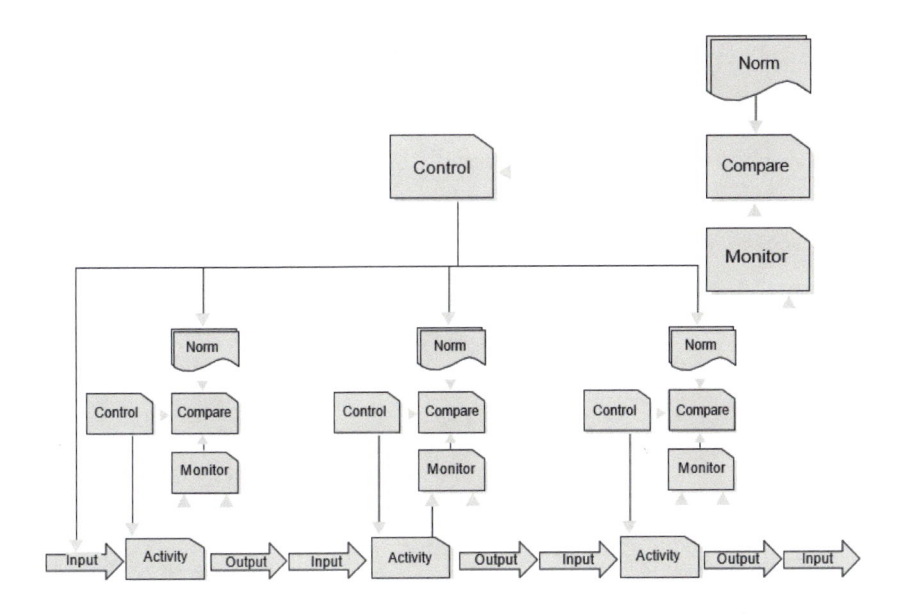

Figure 5.6 The complex monitoring/control cycle

Figure 5.6 shows a **complex monitoring/control cycle:** a process that consists of three important activities. Each activity has an input and output and in turn this output is the input for the next activity. Every activity is controlled by its own monitoring/control cycle with the aid of a series of norms for that specific activity. A co-ordinating monitoring/control cycle monitors the entire process and ensures that all norms are suitable and are being complied with.

The monitoring/control cycle concept can be used to manage:

> the performance of activities in a process or procedure; in theory every activity and its related output can be measured to ensure that problems in the process are identified before the process is completed
> the effectiveness of the process or procedure as a whole
> the performance of a device or a series of devices

| 191

Answer the following questions to determine how the concept of monitoring/control cycles can be used in service management:

> How do we define what we need to monitor?
> How do we monitor (manually or automated)?
> What is a normal process?
> What do we depend on for a normal process?
> What happens before we receive the input?
> How often do we need to measure?

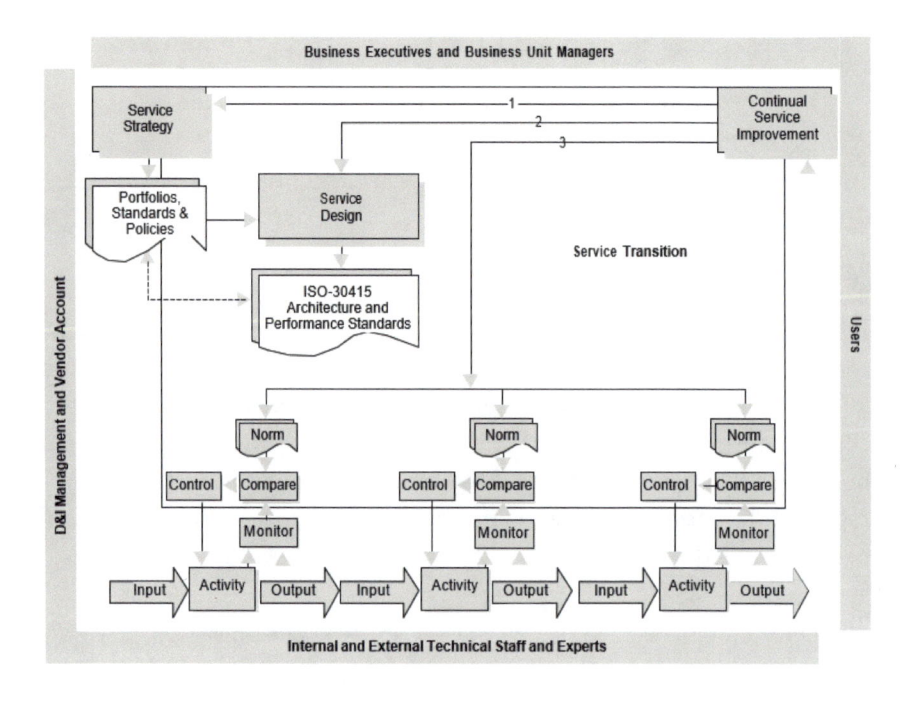

Figure 5.7 The DISM monitoring/control cycle

Figure 5.7 shows an D&I Service Management **monitoring/control cycle** and shows how the control of a process or the components of that process can be used to provide a service.

There are two levels of monitoring:

> **Internal monitoring and control** - focuses on activities and items that take place within a team or department, for instance a D&I manager who monitors the number of projects to determine how many members of the staff affected.
> **External monitoring and control** - the server management team monitors (on behalf of other groups) the CPU performance on important servers and keeps the workload under control; this allows essential applications to perform within the target values set by the application management

This distinction is important. If Service Operation focuses only on internal monitoring the infrastructure is well organized, but the organization has no idea what the quality of the services is or how they can improve this quality. If the organization focuses only on external monitoring it understands how bad the quality of the service is, but it does not know what causes this or how it can change this. In practice, most organizations use a combination of internal and external monitoring, but in many cases they are not linked.

Monitoring without control is irrelevant and ineffective. Monitoring must always be aimed at achieving the service and operational objectives. If, therefore, there is no clear reason for the monitoring of a system or service, there should be no monitoring.

In order for an organization to determine what it wants to monitor, therefore, it must first define the desired outcome: **monitoring and control objectives.** Ideally this process should start with the definition of *Service Level Requirements*. These will specify how the customers and users measure the quality of the service. In addition, these Service Level Requirements provide the input for the Service Design processes.

Availability management, for instance, will determine how the infrastructure must be configured to achieve the fewest possible disruptions.

An important part in determining what Service Operation will be monitoring and how it will get the processes under control is identifying the stakeholders of each service. A stakeholder can be defined as being anyone who has an interest in D&I Services being successfully supplied and received. Each stakeholder will consider, from his own perspective, what is necessary to provide or receive an D&I Service. Service Operation must know what these perspectives are in order to determine what needs to be monitored and what needs to be done with the output.

TOOLS

There are different types of monitoring tools, whereby the situation determines which **type of monitoring** is used:

> Active versus passive monitoring:
> - *Active monitoring* refers to the continuous 'interrogation' of a device or system in order to determine its status.
> - *Passive monitoring* is more commonly known and refers to generating and passing on events to a device or monitoring agent.
>
> Reactive versus proactive monitoring:
> - *Reactive monitoring* is designed to request an action after a certain type of event or disruption.
> - *Proactive monitoring* is used to trace patterns of events that indicate that a system or device may break down. Proactive monitoring is generally used in more mature environments, where these patterns can be detected earlier.
>
> Continuous measuring versus exception-based measuring:
> - *Continuous measuring* is aimed at the real-time monitoring of a system to ensure that it complies with a certain performance norm. As an example, an application server is available 99% of the agreed access time.
> - *Exception-based measuring* does not measure the current performance of a service or system, but discovers and reports exceptions. An example is the generation of an event if a transaction is not completed. It is used for less essential systems or for systems where costs are important.

> **Performance versus output** - There is an important distinction between reporting on the performance of components, teams or a department (*performance*) and reporting that shows that the service quality objectives (*output*) have been achieved. Service Operation carries out both types of monitoring, but ISO-30415 focuses mainly on performance monitoring.

Metrics

It is important that organizations have robust measuring techniques and values that support their objectives. In this context, the following concepts are relevant:

> **Measuring** - refers to all techniques that evaluate the scope, dimension or capacity of an item in relation to a standard or unit. Measuring is only useful when it is possible to measure the actual output of a system, function or process against a standard or desired level. For instance, a server must be capable of processing a minimum of 100 standard transactions per minute.

> **Metrics** - concern the quantitative, periodic evaluation of a process, system or function, together with the procedures and tools that are used for this evaluation, and the procedures for interpreting them. This definition is important because it not only specifies what must be measured, but also how the measuring must be done, what the acceptable lower and upper performance limits are and what actions are necessary in the case of normal performance or an exception.

> **Key Performance Indicators (KPIs)** - refer to a specific, agreed performance level to measure the effectiveness of an organization or process. KPIs are unique to each organization and are related to specific input, output and activities.

5.7 D&I OPERATIONS

Introduction

To deliver the services as agreed with the customer, the service provider will first have to manage the technical infrastructure that is used to deliver the services. If no new customers are added and no new services have to be introduced, if no incidents occur in existing services, and if no changes have to be made in existing services - even then, the D&I organization will be busy with a range of Service Operations. These activities focus on actually delivering the agreed service as agreed.

OPERATIONS BRIDGE

The Operations Bridge is a central point of co-ordination that manages various events and routine operational activities, and reports on the status or performance of technological components.

An Operations Bridge brings together all vital observation points in the D&I infrastructure so that they can be monitored and managed with minimum effort in a central location.

The Operations Bridge combines a great many activities, such as console management, event handling, first line network management and support outside office hours. In some organizations, the D&I Service Desk is a part of the Operations Bridge.

Activities, methods and techniques

JOB SCHEDULING

D&I operations executes standard routines, queries or reports that technical and application management teams have handed over as part of the service or of routine daily maintenance tasks.

BACKUP AND RESTORE

Essentially, backup and restore is a component of good continuity planning. Service Design must therefore ensure that there are good backup strategies for every service. Service Transition must ensure that they are tested in the right way.

Furthermore, some organizations - such as financial service providers and listed companies - must implement and monitor a formal backup and restore strategy as required by the law and regulations. The precise requirements vary per country and industry.

An organization must protect its data, which includes **backup** and storage of data in reserved locations where it is protected and, if necessary, accessible.

A complete backup strategy must be agreed with the business, which must cover the following elements:

> what data should the backup include, and how often must it be made?
> how many generations of data must be retained?
> the backup type and the checkpoints that are used
> the locations used for storage and the rotation schedule
> transport methods
> required tests
> planned recovery point; the point to which data must be recovered after an D&I Service resumes
> planned recovery time; the maximum allowed time to resume an D&I Service after an interruption
> how will it be checked that the backups are functional when they need to be restored?

In all cases, the D&I operations staff must be qualified in backup and restore procedures. These procedures must be documented properly in the procedure manual of D&I operations. Where necessary, you should include specific requirements or targets in OLAs or UCs, and specify user or customer obligations and activities in the relevant SLA.

A **restore** can be initiated from several sources, varying from an event indicating data corruption to a *service request* from a user or customer. A restore may be necessary in case of:

> corrupt service data
> lost service data
> a calamity plan / D&I Service continuity situation
> historical service data required for forensic investigation

PRINT AND OUTPUT

Many services provide their information in **print** or electronic form **(output)**. The service provider must ensure that the information ends up in the right places, correctly and in the right form. Information security often plays a part in this respect.

The customer should notify the service provider in time of a temporarily increased need for print and output.

Laws and regulations may play an important part in print and output. Archiving important or sensitive data is particularly important.

Service providers are generally deemed to be responsible for maintaining the infrastructure to make the print and output available to the customer (printers, storage). In this case, that task must be laid down in the SLA.

5.8 D&I SERVICE DESK

A D&I Service Desk is a **functional unit** with associates involved in differing service events. These service events come in by phone, internet or infrastructure, events which are reported automatically.

The D&I Service Desk is a very important element of the D&I department of an organization. It must be the only contact point for D&I users and it deals with all incidents and service requests. The associates often use software tools to record and manage all events.

Justification and role of a D&I Service Desk

Many organizations consider a D&I Service Desk the best means for a first line support in case of D&I problems. A D&I Service Desk offers the following benefits:

> - improved customer service, better perception of the service on the part of the client and greater client satisfaction
> - greater access through one single contact, communication and information point
> - client and user requests are resolved better and quicker
> - improved co-operation and communication
> - less negative impact on business
> - better managed and controlled infrastructure
> - better use of resources through D&I support and increased productivity of company associates
> - more meaningful management information for decisions concerning support

D&I Service Desk objectives

The primary purpose of the D&I Service Desk is to resume 'normal service' to the user as soon as possible. This may be resolving a technical error, but also filling a service request or answering a question.

Organizational structure of a D&I Service Desk

There are many ways to organize a D&I Service Desk. The solution will be different for each organization. The most important options are:

> local D&I Service Desk
> centralized D&I Service Desk
> virtual D&I Service Desk
> 24-hour service
> specialized D&I Service Desk groups

These options are elaborated further below. In practice, an organization will implement a structure that combines a number of these options in order to satisfy the needs of the business.

The **local D&I Service Desk** is located at or physically close to the users it is supporting. Because of this, communications are often much smoother and the visible presence is attractive for some users. However, a local D&I Service Desk is expensive and may be inefficient if the amount of service events does not really justify a D&I Service Desk.

There may be a few sound reasons for maintaining a local D&I Service Desk:

> linguistic, cultural and political differences
> different time zones
> specialized groups of users
> existence of adjusted or special services for which specialized knowledge is required
> status of the users

The number of D&I Service Desks can be reduced by installing them at one single location, software workflow system, or by reducing the number of local D&I Service Desks. In that case, the associates are assigned to one or more **centralized D&I Service Desk** structures. This may be less expensive and more efficient, because fewer associates can deal with the service events (calls), while the level of knowledge of the D&I Service Desk is bound to increase.

By using technology, specifically the internet, and the use of support tools, it is possible to create the impression of a centralized D&I Service Desk, whereas the associates are in fact spread out over a number of geographic or structural locations: this is the **virtual D&I Service Desk.**

Some international organizations like to combine two or more geographically spread out D&I Service Desks in order to offer a **24/7 service**. In this way, a D&I Service Desk in Asia, for example, can deal with incoming service events during standard office hours, whereby at the end of that period, a D&I Service Desk in Europe takes care of any outstanding events. That desk deals with those service events together with its own events and at the end of the day, responsibility is transferred to a D&I Service Desk in America, which then returns responsibility to the Asian D&I Service Desk, thus completing the cycle.

It may be attractive for some organizations to create specialized **D&I Service Desk groups**, so that incidents relating to a specific D&I Service are routed straight to the specialized group. In this way, incidents can be resolved more promptly.

The **environment** of the D&I Service Desk must be carefully selected, preferably a location where workstations have adequate space with natural light. A quiet environment with good acoustics is equally important, because the associates should not be bothered by each other's telephone conversations. Ergonomic office furniture is also important.

D&I Service Desk personnel

Care should be taken that a sufficient **number of associates** are available, so that the D&I Service Desk can meet the business demand at any time. The number of service events can, of course, strongly fluctuate from day-to-day and hour to hour. An organization will take peak hours and quiet periods into account.

A decision should be made as to which skill levels are necessary for the D&I Service Desk personnel. To determine the required **skill level**, weigh the arranged resolution times against the complexity of the supported systems, and 'the outlay the business is willing to pay'. The optimal and most efficient approach is generally a first line support via the D&I Service Desk, which records the service event and transmits escalations promptly to more expert second-level and third-level support groups.

If the skill levels have been established, the D&I Service Desk must be directed in a way that the associates receive and maintain the necessary skills. During all work hours, there has to be a good mix of skills present.

It is essential that all D&I Service Desk associates receive sufficient **training.** All new associates must follow a formal introduction program. The precise content of it will vary with each new associate, subject to the existing expertise and experience.

In order to keep the D&I Service Desk associates up-to-date, a program is necessary so that they can be kept informed of new developments, services and techniques. The timing of these type of activities is essential, because they should not impact the normal tasks. Many D&I Service Desks organize short training sessions during quiet periods when the associates are handling fewer service events.

It is very important that all D&I associates realize the importance of the D&I Service Desk and the people working there. A considerable attrition of associates has a disturbing effect and can lead to an incoherent service. Thus the managers have to engage in efforts **to retain the associates**.

Many organizations find it meaningful to appoint a number of so-called **super users** in the user community. They function as contact persons with the D&I organization in general and the D&I Service Desk in particular.

Organizations can provide the super users extra training and use them as communication channel. They can be asked to filter requests and certain problems on behalf of the user community. If an important service or component is down, causing an extra burden for many users, this may lead to many reactions coming in.

Super users do not provide support for the entire D&I. In many cases, the super user will offer support only for a specific application, module or business unit. As a business user a super user often has thorough knowledge of important company processes and knows how services are working in practice. It is very useful to share this with the D&I Service Desk, so that it can offer better quality services in the future.

Metrics

In order to evaluate the performance of the D&I Service Desk at regular time intervals, **metrics** must be established. In this way, the maturity, efficiency, effectiveness and potentials can be established and the D&I Service Desk actions improved.

Metrics for the performance of a D&I Service Desk must be selected carefully and realistically. It is common to select those metrics which are readily available and which point to a possible indicator for the performance. However, this can be misleading. The total number of service events that a D&I Service Desk has received, for example, is not an indicator by itself of a good or bad performance, and can, in fact, be caused by events which do not impact on the D&I Service Desk.

In order to determine this, further analysis and more detailed metrics are necessary which are researched for a certain period of time. Besides the statistics mentioned earlier regarding the handling of service events, the metrics consist, among others of:

> first line handling time; the percentage of service events, which are resolved by the first level, without the necessity to escalate to other support groups
> average time to resolve an incident (or other type of service call) (if it is resolved by the first level)
> average time to escalate an incident (if a first line solution is not possible)

- average handling costs of an incident
- percentage of client and user updates which are executed within the target values, as set forth in the SLA objectives
- average time to evaluate and close out a resolved incident

Besides following 'hard' metrics in the performance of the D&I Service Desk, it is also important to carry out 'soft' metrics: **the Client and User Satisfaction Surveys** (eg Do clients [employees] think that their concerns are being acknowledges or remedied. Was the D&I Service Desk associate friendly and empathetic?). User or client can best complete this type of metrics, but specific questions about the D&I Service Desk itself may also be asked.

Outsourcing the D&I Service Desk

The decision to contract out or outsource is a strategic subject for Senior Managers and is discussed in detail in Chapter 4 (Service Strategy and Service Design).

Regardless of the reasons for outsourcing or the size of the outsource contract, it is important that the organization remains responsible for the activities and services rendered by the D&I Service Desk. The organization is ultimately responsible for the outcome of the decision and must therefore decide which service is going to be offered.

If the D&I Service Desk is being outsourced, the **tools** must be consistent with the tools being used by the organizations client. Outsourcing is frequently seen as a chance to replace obsolescent or inadequate tools; however, serious integration problems often arise between the new and existing tools and processes.

Ideally, the D&I Service Desk being outsourced must use the same **tools and processes** to enable a smooth process stream between the D&I Service Desk and the second and third level support groups.

The **SLA targets** for incident handling and handling times must be arranged with the clients and between all teams and departments; OLA and underlying contract objectives must be co- ordinated and in tune with separate support groups, so that they support the SLA targets.

Most companies are a long way from deploying a service desk in 2021.

INDEXING

- 171 D&I elements, 25
- 24/7 service, 201
- 27 diversity types, 19, 26, 28, 29
- 32 D&I domains, 19, 25
- 4 D&I categories, 25

A

- absenteeism, 31
- accent bias, 35
- access management, 184-188
  granting rights, 186
  verification, 186
- accommodation, 30, 51
- accountability, 27, 51, 56, 58-60, 105, 118
- accountability for actions, 56
- acquisition, 71, 107
- active monitoring, 194
- ad hoc, 109, 114
- advocacy, 31, 57, 60
- ageism (see negative feelings), 36, 37
- alert mechanism, 160
- alumni associations, 90
- amalgamations, 69
- American population, 40
- ancillary bodies, 90
- anomalies, 79
- anti-nepotism policy, 43
- apprenticeship, 71
- Asperger's syndrome, 30

B

- baby boomers, 36
- Balanced Scorecard (see BSC), 131
- baseline data, 64, 118
- benchmarking, 122, 126, 129-131
  process maturity comparison, 130
  Total Cost of Ownership (see TCO), 131, 183
- Bennett-Alexander, Dawn, 14
- best practice, 18
- biological sex, 38-40
- biometric information, 187
- Brache, Alan, 133
- brainstorming, 179
- British Standards Institute (see BSI), 18
- bureau of labor statistics, 40
- Business Impact Analysis (see BIA), 100
- business model, 14
- Business Relationship Managers (see BRM), 96
- Business Service Management (see BSM), 101
- Business Unit (see BU), 96, 103, 104

C

- Capability Maturity Model Integration (see CMMI), 108, 115
- cari dominguez, 15
- Carobolante, Lorelei, 16
- case law, 14
- centralized D&I service desk, 200-201
- cessation of employment, 69, 82, 83
- chamber, 104, 105, 148
- Change Advisory Board (see CAB), 124
- charter, 98
- chatgpt, 115
- cheek kisses, 33
- chief executive, 105
- childcare vouchers, 51
- chronological analysis, 179
- citizenship status, 36, 37, 42, 43
- client portfolio, 96
- co-convener, 16
- cobit, 185
- cognitive abilities, 28
- cognitive approaches, 65
- cognitive different-abilities, 30
- cognitive disabilities, 30
  dyslexia, 30, 31, 32
  ADHD, 30
  dyspraxia, 30, 31
- commitment, 26, 48, 52, 56, 58, 62-65, 73, 80, 89, 108, 112, 118, 125
- communication, 12, 33, 57, 60, 64, 89, 111, 117, 128, 134, 136, 138, 140, 141, 199, 202
- compassion, 75
- compliance, 50, 185
- Component Failure Impact Analysis (see CFIA), 147
- Configuration Item (see CI), 100
- Configuration Management System (see CMS), 102, 135, 167, 168, 181
- consultations, 86, 87
- Continual Service Improvement (see CSI), 119, 120
- continuous measuring, 194
- control cycle, 190-192
    closed cycle systems, 190
    open cycle systems, 190
- convener, 16
- conviction, 44, 75
- corpus, 14
- cost effectiveness, 119
- CPU performance, 193
- criminal background, 29, 44
- critical success factor, 141
- Critical Success Factors (see CSF), 103, 141, 152, 169, 173
- CSI approaches,
  functional approach, 137
  lifecycle approach, 137
  service approach, 137
- cultural background, 29, 33, 42
- cultural traits, 34
- cultures, 33, 38, 105
    customs, 33, 35
    language, 5, 6, 14, 28, 35, 76, 115, 137
    religion, 28, 33, 52, 54
    traditional foods, 33

D

- D&I Infrastructure Library (See DIIL), 19
- D&I Service Continuity Management (see DISCM), 100, 150, 151, 182
- D&I Service Desk, 102, 121, 146, 150, 161, 163, 166, 167, 169, 172, 173, 176, 181, 184, 196, 199-204
- D&I Service Management Field (see DISMF), 10, 17
- data extraction, 26, 27, 148
    - demographic data, 27, 59, 67, 69, 87
    - sentiment analysis, 27, 28
    - market data, 27
- data warehousing, 107
- decision-making framework, 96
- demand management, 12, 151
- demographic data, 27, 59, 67, 69, 87
- demographic of wage, 13
- diagnosis, 163, 166, 167, 176, 179-181
- disabilities, 30, 31, 51
- disability equality index, 31
- disenfranchised population, 105
- DISM forum (see D&I service management)
- dismissals, 83
- disparate impact, 77
- disproportionate, 67, 70
- diverse population, 13
- Diversity & Inclusion (see D&I), 5, 6, 16, 115
- Diversity & Inclusion Professionals (see DIPS), 19
- DNA, 187
- dynamic adoption, 18
- educated women, 13

E

- Employee Resource Group (see ERG), 31
- Employee Resource Groups (see ERG's), 52, 66
- employment law, 14
- end-to-end, 146, 147
- enterprise, 96
- Equal Employment Opportunity Commission (see EEOC), 15, 30
- equality, 17, 31, 48, 53, 56, 60
- equity, 5, 13, 28, 48, 53, 56, 60, 70, 79
- ergonomic office, 201
- error messages, 135, 160,
- escalates, 166
    - functional escalation, 166
    - hierarchical escalation, 166
- ethical considerations, 14, 65
- ethnicity, 28, 35, 41, 42
    - Hispanic, 35
    - Irish, 35
    - Jewish, 35
- ethnodiversity, 28
- European Foundation for Quality Management (see EFQM), 108
- event correlation, 156
- exam bodies, 19
- exception-based measuring, 194
- exorbitant costs, 41
- expatriation, 81, 82
- expensive legislation, 133
- External Infrastructure (see EI), 28
    - gifting & philanthropy, 28
    - joining minority chambers, 28
    - marketing campaigns, 28
- extroverts, 33

F

- fairness, 41, 48, 53, 56, 60, 61, 68, 78, 79, 81, 82
- Fault Tree Analysis (see FTA), 147
- feasible goals, 140
- felony convictions, 44
- finance suite, 165
- financial authorisation, 172
- fingerprints, 187
- foreign-born workers, 36
- forms of whistle, 14
- frameworks, 11, 108, 117, 123
- French culture, 33
- functional diversity, 46
- functional unit, 199

G

- gap analysis, 131
- Gartner, 110, 131
- Gates, Bill, 30
- generation xers, 36
- Generative Pre-trained Transformer (see ChatGPT), 115
- genetic sex spectrum, 39
- geographic location, 28
- geographical location, 34, 37, 41, 43
- glass ceiling, 38
- global consensus, 6, 14
  - iso-30415 standard, 14, 17, 19, 61
- global guidance standard, 17
- global workforce mobility, 69
- governance, 11, 25, 49, 50, 56, 58, 64, 67, 90, 96
- government alliances, 14

- grievances, 29, 64, 65, 67
- Grow The Business (see GTB), 98

H

- harassment, 56, 66, 73, 104
- Henderson, Effenus, 16
- heritage, 35
- HIPAA, 185
- HR officer, 105
- human capital, 56, 69
- human resources, 14-16, 25, 29, 68, 103, 104, 105, 154, 186, 187
- Human Resources Management Lifecycle (see HRMLC), 68
- human resources practices, 14
- human rights campaign's guide, 39
- human variation, 31
  - deficit hyperactivity disorder, 31
  - autistic spectrum, 31
  - dyscalculia, 31
  - dyspraxia, 30, 31
  - tourette syndrome, 31

I

- ideologies, 34, 37,
- ill-defined, 174
- Immigration Reform and Control Act (see IRCA), 36
- immigration status, 36
- impartial process, 77
- implementation, 11, 18, 20, 61-63, 67, 82, 91, 102, 118, 125, 126, 131, 136, 140, 142, 145, 151, 159, 169, 173, 183, 184, 188
- implementation phase, 126

- incarcerated, 44
- incentivize, 6, 18
- incident registration, 163, 167, 176
- inclusion corporation (see inclusion score incorporated), 19
- inclusion equity, 13, 28
- Inclusion Maturity Model Integration (see IMMI), 112
- inclusion process, 53
- inclusive organizational culture, 60, 64, 65, 66
- inclusiveness, 49, 52, 53, 75, 85, 87, 88
- income-based laws, 41
- induction, 54, 72, 73, 74
- inpatriation, 81, 82
- institutional, 14
- instrumentation, 160
- integration of demographics, 14
- intellectual functioning level, 30
- interfaces, 101, 142, 158, 159, 167, 172, 174, 181, 187
- internal infrastructure, 26, 27, 105
    business resource groups, 27, 52
    employee resource groups, 27, 52, 55, 59, 66, 104
    internal advisory boards, 27
- International Organization for Standards (see ISO), 5, 6, 16, 26
- international standard, 48-50
- intersectionality, 54, 57, 59, 65, 70
- intersex, 39
- intrinsic value, 56
- introverts, 33
- inventory, 98, 139
- investor management, 122
- Ishikawa diagrams, 179

- ISO 10667 assessment service delivery, 50
- ISO 30400 vocabulary, 50
- ISO 30405 guidelines on recruitment, 50
- ISO 30408 guidelines on human governance, 50
- ISO 9000 (iso-9000:2000), 110
- ISO 9000 series, 117
- ISO/DIS 30415:2021, 112

J

- job accommodation network, 30
- justice, 5, 118

K

- kaizen principle, 108
- keith institute, 18
- kepner-tregoe, 179
- Key Performance Indicators (see KPIs), 195
- known error, 166, 175, 180, 181
- Known Error Database (see KEDB), 175, 181
- KPMG's World Class IT Maturity Model, 110

L

- labor intensive, 128
- labor union membership, 46
- lack-of-inclusion, 113

- learning and development, 54, 64, 67, 69, 73-77, 81
- legal dockets, 29
- levels in CMMI,
    - defined process, 109, 118
    - incomplete process, 109
    - managed process, 109
    - optimizing process, 109
    - performed process, 109
    - quantitatively managed process, 109
- LGBTQ chamber of commerce, 104
- LGBTQIA+, 40
- lilly ledbetter fair pay act, 41
- linguistics, 30, 34
- local D&I service desk, 200

M

- management status, 47, 48
- managerial awareness, 75
- mannerism, 32, 39
- marital status, 29, 43
- marketing, 28, 71, 95, 97, 187
- maturity ladder, 107
- measurement phase, 126
- member-parts, 14
- mental health, 28, 31, 42
- menu selection, 171
- micro-aggression, 66
- micro-identification, 13
- military experience, 44
- millennials care, 36
- mitigate bias, 75, 83
- morals, 37, 38, 45
- multi-national corporations, 14
- mutual dependency, 101
- mutual respect, 64

N

- national origin, 14, 34, 52, 54
- National Science Foundation (see NSF), 18
- national symposium, 31
- neurodiversity, 28, 31
- Nolan, Richard, 107
- non-binary gender identities, 38
    - demigender, 39
    - gender fluid, 39
    - gender queer,
    - gender-transition, 38
    - transgender, 38
- Non-Governmental Organizations (see NGO), 49
- non-pay elements, 51
- norms off guard, 14

O

- Obama's fair chances business pledge (2016), 44
- occupational federations, 90
- onboarding, 69, 72, 73, 74
- openai, 115
- Operational Level Agreements (see OLAs), 162
- operations bridge, 196
- organizational,
    - culture, 7, 12, 31-33, 37, 46, 47, 53, 58, 59, 63-66, 71, 105, 116, 118, 138, 151
    - governance, 11, 49, 56, 58, 64, 67, 90, 96

- hierarchy, 43, 47, 100
- leadership, 47, 56, 58, 59, 64, 65, 76, 90
- organizations, 14, 15, 17, 18, 29, 48, 49, 51, 56, 63, 65, 70, 71, 73, 75, 77, 78, 80, 81, 83, 85, 86, 88, 89, 91, 99, 101, 107, 108, 114-116, 125, 127-130, 133, 171, 172, 184, 187, 193, 195, 197, 199, 201, 202, 204
  - for-profit, 14, 91
  - non-profit, 14
  - governments, 14
- outcomes, 49, 51, 56, 58, 60, 62, 63, 65, 69, 71, 73, 75, 77-82, 84, 86, 87, 89, 91, 92

- present assets, 129
- privilege, 42
- problem management, 147, 150, 151, 164, 168, 174-178, 181-184
  - proactive, 51, 101, 135, 140, 144, 151, 176, 194
  - reactive, 114, 176, 194
- problem registration, 176, 177, 181,
- problem-solving abilities, 30
- process owner, 119-121, 124
- procurement process, 88, 89
- product delivery, 25
- purchase order system, 165

P

- P-D-C-A cycle, 137
- paid leave, 51
- pain value analysis, 179
- parental status, 29, 43
- pareto analysis, 179
- passive monitoring, 194
- pay and benefits, 51, 69, 78, 79
- Paycheck Fairness Act (see PFA), 41
- perceived inequalities, 26
- personal data, 7, 13, 27, 29
- personal ethos, 34
- philanthropic, 90
- planning phase, 126
- political beliefs, 29, 45
- polling, 155
- Post Implementation Review (see PIR), 142
- pregnant women, 43
- prejudice, 60

Q

- queer, 6, 39, 105

R

- race, 35, 41
- alaska native, 35
- Asian, 35, 201
- black or African, 35
- native Hawaiian, 35
- white, 6, 10, 35
- RACI matrix (see Responsible, Accountable, Consulted, Informed), 118
- rationalize, 98
- realistic schedule, 140
- reap, 108
- recruitment, 34, 38, 42, 46, 50, 69, 71, 72, 75, 78, 81
- recruitment content, 42

- red tape, 171
- redeployment, 69, 82, 83
- redundancies, 83
- refactor, 98
- refinements, 16
- refrains, 155
- religious affiliations, 45
- relocation, 81, 82
- remedial, 83
- repatriation, 81, 82
- reproductive organs, 39
- Request For Change (see RFC), 151, 158, 186
- resignation, 83
- restore, 197, 198
- retaliation, 14, 46, 56, 66, 73
- retaliation prevention, 56
- retention, 49, 52, 66, 67, 78, 82, 116
- retirement, 41, 69, 79, 82, 83, 186
- Return On Investment (see ROI), 138
- right-to-work, 46
- robust evidence, 59
- romantic, 40
- rudimentary, 104
- Rummler, Geary, 133
- Run The Business (see RTB), 98

S

- secondments, 81, 82
- segregated, 38, 39
- senior managers, 166, 204
- service catalogs, 12, 27
- Service Catalogue Management (see SCM), 99
    - business service catalogue, 100, 102
    - technical service catalogue, 101, 102
- service delivery, 12, 50, 87, 93, 135, 144
- service design, 11, 12, 20, 122, 124, 142, 145, 146, 150, 182, 186, 193, 197, 204
- service design phase,
- Service Failure Analysis (see SFA), 147
- Service Knowledge Management System (see SKMS), 102, 181
- Service Level Agreements (see SLAS), 119
- Service Level Management (see SLM), 137, 142, 168
- service lifecycle, 11, 20, 119, 142, 144
    - design, 11, 12, 26, 27, 29, 31, 51, 65, 75, 82, 91, 99, 110, 124, 144, 146, 150, 158, 160, 186, 193, 197
    - improvement, 62, 68, 83, 102, 107-109, 112, 115, 118-121, 123, 124, 129, 130, 131, 134, 135, 137, 138, 140-146, 149, 150, 151, 189
    - operation, 20, 121, 131, 137, 142, 145, 146, 147, 150, 154, 168, 176, 186, 193-195
    - strategy, 11, 12, 52, 62, 64, 91, 92, 97, 100, 122, 124-126, 144, 146, 149, 150, 186, 197, 204
    - transition, 11, 60, 61, 82, 83, 121, 145, 150, 197
- service manager, 119, 120-122, 149
- service operation, 20, 121, 137, 142, 145-147, 150, 154, 176, 186, 193-195
- service operation life phase, 121

213

- service owner, 119-121, 123, 124, 147
- Service Portfolio Management (see SPM), 12, 96
- service request, 135, 170, 171-173, 187, 198, 199
- service strategy, 11, 12, 20, 100, 144, 146, 149, 150, 183, 186, 204
- service strategy phase, 100
- service transition, 11, 20, 121, 145, 150, 151, 181, 182, 197
- sex, 38, 39, 43
- sex characteristics, 39
- sexual attraction, 40
- sexual orientation, 40, 41, 43, 52, 54
- six sigma, 108
- skill level, 201, 202
- Society for Human Resources Management (see SHRM), 14, 15
- socioeconomic status, 29, 34, 37, 42, 43
- Socioeconomic Status (see SES), 42
- software, 107, 108, 134, 136, 148, 155, 160, 167, 170, 180, 199, 200
- Software Capability Maturity Model (see SW-CMM), 108
- Software Engineering Institute (see SEI), 108
- solicited, 64, 67, 83, 84, 87
- sox, 185
- specialized D&I service desk, 200, 201
- staged model, 107, 108
- stakeholders, 14, 17, 51, 53, 54, 58, 61, 62, 64-66, 88, 90-92, 104, 105, 139, 194
- human resources, 14-16, 29, 68, 103, 105, 154, 186, 187
- procurement, 29, 63, 88, 89, 105, 173
- product, 25, 85-87, 96, 105

- stereotypes, 32, 36, 38, 43
- stereotypical language, 76
- strategic objectives, 52, 58, 60, 61, 63, 65, 69-71, 73-75, 77-81, 83, 86, 88, 89, 91, 92
- succession planning, 69, 79, 80, 81
- super users, 202, 203
- supplier diversity, 29, 55, 88, 103
- suss out, 47
- sustainable success, 14
- swim lanes, 133
- SWOT-analysis (see Strength, Weakness, Opportunities and Threats), 131
- Systems Improvement Plan (see SIP), 119

T

- tactics, 61
- Tajiri, Satoshi, 30
- talent pool, 79
- tax breaks, 44
- Technical Committee (see TC), 16
- Technical Observation Post (see TOP), 149
- technical staff, 161
- thirty-two domains of diversity and inclusion, 48
- thought-style, 32, 33
- threats, 131, 133
- time zones, 200
- title VII of the civil rights act of 1964, 14
- tools for CSI,
    automated incident and problem solving, 135
    business intelligence, 136

- event management, 135, 153, 154, 155, 157, 159, 168
- financial management, 12, 122, 136, 146, 183
- knowledge management, 102, 123, 124, 135, 141, 150, 151, 159, 181
- performance management, 69, 76-78, 135
- project and portfolio management, 136
- service request processing, 135
- software test management, 136
- software version management, 135
- statistical analysis instruments, 135
- system and network management, 135
- top-down changes, 108
- training,
  - bias training, 27
  - continued education, 27
  - cultural training, 27
- Transform The Business (see TTB), 98
- transparency, 56, 60, 68, 78
- trend analysis (see organization), 134, 136
- trigger, 158
- Trump's first step act (2018), 44
- typical rights, 185

U

- umbrella organization, 17
- unconscious bias, 36, 41, 44, 48
- Underpinning Contracts (see UCs), 143, 162
- unequivocally, 98
- ungender identities, 39
  - agender, 39
  - gender-free, 39
  - genderless, 39
  - non-gendered, 39
- union affiliation, 46
- united states census bureau, 34
- united states of america, 4, 13, 29
- unsolicited feedback, 64, 67, 83, 84, 87
- upper-level jobs, 40

V

- Value On Investment (see VOI), 139
- vendor management, 122
- virtual D&I service desk, 200, 201
- visual aids, 31
- visual comprehension, 30

W

- waterfall, 131
- Watson, Emma, 30
- western world, 13, 14
- whistle blowing, 14, 61, 73
- work councils, 50, 55, 66, 86, 87
- workaholics, 36
- workforce mobility, 69, 81, 82
- workforce segmentation, 69, 70
  - employee-based segmentation, 69
  - role-based segmentation, 69

| 215

- working group, 15, 16
    - competencies for top diversity professionals, 16
    - diversity metrics, 16
    - focused on diversity programs, 16

X

- X chromosomes, 39

Y

- Y chromosomes, 39

Z

- Zeithaml, 132

Made in the USA
Columbia, SC
22 October 2024